ORTHODOX SYNTHESIS
THE UNITY OF THEOLOGICAL THOUGHT

ORTHODOX SYNTHESIS
THE UNITY
OF
THEOLOGICAL THOUGHT

An anthology published in commemoration of the fifteenth anniversary of Metropolitan Philip as Primate of the Antiochian Orthodox Christian Archdiocese of North America.

JOSEPH J. ALLEN
Editor

ST. VLADIMIR'S SEMINARY PRESS
CRESTWOOD, NEW YORK
1981

Library of Congress Cataloging in Publication Data
Main entry under title:

Orthodox synthesis.

Includes bibliographical references.
1. Theology, Eastern church—Addresses, essays,
lectures. 2. Philip, Metropolitan. I. Allen,
Joseph J.,   II. Philip, Metropolitan.
BX320.2.076   230'.19   81-5674
ISBN 0-913836-84-2   AACR2

© Copyright 1981

by

ST. VLADIMIR'S SEMINARY PRESS

ALL RIGHTS RESERVED

ISBN 0-913836-84-2

PRINTED IN THE UNITED STATES OF AMERICA
BY
ATHENS PRINTING COMPANY
461 Eighth Avenue
New York, NY 10001

The writers of these pages call the readers—and especially you, Philip—to come and drink a new drink:

Δεῦτε πόμα πίωμεν καινόν!

(Paschal Canon)

Contents

Preface

The title and writers in this book are not arbitrarily chosen. Both bear special significance to the meaning and task of the Eastern Orthodox faith in our contemporary age.

Not only those in the Orthodox Church, but also (and especially) the non-Orthodox will find in these pages a true "synthesis" of central concepts and concerns as creatively expressed by some of the leading Orthodox professors in their respective fields. One will find not only tangential forms, however, but a common foundation—a "unity of theological thought"—out of which each comes and which ties all of the writers together.

The title and writers are also significantly related to Metropolitan Philip, to whom this book is dedicated. Although the title "Orthodox Synthesis" will be explained in the first chapter, we might say here of the writers that they are found in the arena of Orthodoxy in America and in Antioch, both of which Philip has remained devoted to throughout his ministry as priest and bishop. To put such names together, needless to say, is a great honor paid to Philip on his fifteenth anniversary as Metropolitan Archbishop of the Antiochian Orthodox Christian Archdiocese of North America. It is also a great honor to me, as editor, and I remain indebted to each one.

JOSEPH J. ALLEN
Editor

CHAPTER 1

THE ORTHODOX SYNTHESIS

There are many things which we do not know. But one thing we know for certain is that this world is imperfect. However, beyond the imperfection, the trials and tribulations, the sorrow, the tears and the agony of this world, there is a perfect world.

Metropolitan Philip

The word synthesis (from συντίθημι, "put together") aptly describes the various facets of the theology, history, and ethos of the Orthodox Church. This will become apparent as the reader notes such facets emerging in the following pages. More particularly, the synthesis in the Church (as found in these pages) means a "coming together" in various ways: of God and man, of man and man, of theory and practice, of interpretation and proclamation, of Church and state. It is a word which has sprung from the lips of Philip at those spontaneous moments when he seems to sense the depth of the words of the proskomedia: "Blessed is the union of Thy holy things" (τὴν ἁγίαν ἕνωσιν—the holy union).

It is essential, however, that before exploring these various facets of the synthesis of Orthodoxy we understand the theological sense of our very existence. All the chapters which follow in this book can be subsumed under this basic understanding, which we shall attempt to make clear in this first chapter.

J. J. A.

The Meaning of Synthesis: An Introduction to the Term

by

JOSEPH J. ALLEN

Existence in the Orthodox *modus vivendi* has its roots in a living unity and harmony—a true *synthesis*—of subject and object. Humankind is limited, conditioned, dependent, relative, and in the deepest sense, *caused*. God is, on the other hand, He who is unlimited, perfect, absolute, eternally the same, the *still point* of this existence; indeed, He is the *Causer* of all life. The human, as *homo religiosus*, begins his growth into this ongoing synthesis from this point; the human *experience* of this world finds meaning in this order and harmony in which he sees himself as a distinctive part.

This does not put humanity, as some recent "process theologians" of the West propose, in a deprived position. Rather, he is now able to move, create, indeed to be a *causer* himself, because he knows *from* where he begins. For the Orthodox, the idea of creation implies a duality of existence: God and creature, who is brought into that existence by a loving freedom, pure and absolute, *ex mera libertate*. The unchanging *still point* which God is, does not mean that He is uninvolved in human lives; nothing could be more un-Orthodox than such a teaching. After all, He has "pitched His tent among us," and thus is, at once, always *with* us, and always *coming* to us. The *still point* of this synthesis is God's nature or essence (οὐσία), which is in no way man's nature or essence. What man shares is God's energy (ἐνέργεια), in which God

13

has given Himself from the moment He breathed life into
the dust. But there is—and this is crucial for understanding
the synthesis of human existence—a difference between God's
essence and energy. It is the energy which is ours to have—
and it always comes *ad extra*.

Creation has other implications vis-à-vis this synthesis.
God calls creation "out of nothing" (ἐξ οὐκ ὄντων) to be
a new creation, which becomes the bearer and carrier of His
very image or idea (His icon), and yet without ever being
existentially identified with it, the result being precisely a
confusion in the *order* of that synthesis. A human cannot
merely say of himself, "I am who I am"—that is, that one
exists by some "right of nature." In short, Orthodoxy will
say that we do not exist by some sort of intrinsic cause or
nature of our own, but solely by the grace of the Causer.

The central event of this synthesis, intimately connected
with *creation* itself (in which God "gives" Himself to both
humankind and the cosmos) is the *incarnation* of Jesus Christ.
Since that time (and after the many councils, e.g., Chalcedon,
which tried to clarify just what the incarnation means) the
whole of this Orthodox synthesis can be called *incarnational*.
This is true in the sense that the truth and love of God, as
"fleshed out" in the person of Christ, must be for us, in our
own lives, "fleshed out." If anything has marked the thrust
of the Antiochian school, it has been this *incarnational*—and
thus existential—approach. While this certainly was not the
exclusive thrust of Antioch, it can be seen most clearly in the
Antiochian-Alexandrian dialectic of the fourth century—and
it even led some to various heresies! But it has nevertheless
remained central to the Antiochian approach—and certainly
has manifested itself in all that for which Philip has struggled
over the years.

But with the incarnation we find the *paradox* of all time—
one which only describes the *meaning* of the God-man synthesis: perfection engages imperfection, eternity becomes a
child. Never before was I so aware of the profundity of this
God-man paradox as when my study of this term *synthesis*
(which includes the writers in this book) revealed that paradox. Why should God exchange heaven for earth, the stars

for the cave, glory for poverty? It was only after this study that I came to understand—with my *heart*—the answer. This discovery was only further clarified as I chanted the Akathist hymn to the Theotokos (who is so central to our understanding of the incarnation), which included such phrases that are attributed to the great hymnographer, St. Romanos the Melodist. Is it not fitting that one such as this, born out of the womb of Syria and Beirut (so well known to Philip), could so beautifully capture the paradox of this synthesis?

Referring to the willing act of the Theotokos, Romanos first proclaims the mysterious nature of this paradox: "Hail, thou height untrod by human minds; Hail, thou depth hard to scan, even for angels' eyes," and then, "Hail, thou through whom Creation is renewed; Hail, thou through whom the Creator becomes a babe!" After that, the paradox leads the Theotokos to respond, "To my soul thy message seems hard to grasp; how speakest thou of a virgin conception?" (oikoi 1 and 2).

How difficult for Joseph, who represents our most human and logical response, to understand this paradoxical synthesis: "Floods of doubtful thoughts troubled the wise Joseph within, and he feared a furtive love as he beheld thee unwed, O Blameless One" (oikos 6). But even more revealing: "Hail, thou who makest things differ to agree; Hail, thou who joinest together virginity and motherhood!" (oikos 15). And for no other reason does this paradoxical synthesis exist except as it is described in the same hymn: "Hail, Guide of the wisdom of the faithful; Hail, Joy of all generations" (oikos 9). And finally, and most clearly connecting the *paradox* with our *salvation*: "Hail, healing of my body; Hail, salvation of my soul!" (oikos 23).

But if anywhere, it is in the Nativity hymns of the incarnation that the same Romanos calls up the salvation-granting paradox: timelessness takes on time, history becomes today, the Logos takes on flesh, God stoops to lift man. The synthesis, he tells us in one Nativity kontakion, is indeed a paradoxical one: "Behold, the Father is His daughter's son!" God is human, and is, of all things, a *babe* born in a cave; a cave surrendered by the earth precisely in order for this synthesis to be realized! He who is "our God before all ages [time], assumes the form of a newborn babe" (Pre-Nativity kontakion).

Because He is all this, Christ is, finally, τὸ δῶρον τῶν δώρων, "the gift of gifts" who becomes one of us, that we might be one of His. But this paradoxical synthesis is only driven deeper into the Christian heart by that other Syrian hymnographer, St. John of Damascus, rightly called "streaming with gold" (χρυσορρόας). However, with him we look to the other side of the same paradox, that is, the "other birth," the Anastasis, the Pascha, in which Life itself should die, to defeat death. "Thou who in Thy birth didst not break the virgin bars—Thou hast now opened for us the gates of paradise." And in another place: "Let us proceed with lighted candles to Christ, who goes forth from the tomb like a Bridegroom" (Paschal Canon). In this incarnational-resurrectional paradox is that synthesis which realizes our salvation and for which we can do no less than ask Jerusalem, which eternally represents the world, to shine: "Shine! Shine, O New Jerusalem, for the glory of the Lord has risen upon thee!" (Paschal Canon).

This, then, is the synthesis of the God who became the child, τὸ παιδίον, but who also is ὁ πρὸ αἰώνων θεὸς—a paradox upon which hinges all that which is written in the pages to follow.

If we mention America and Antioch, Creator and creature, incarnation and resurrection, as part of the meaning of this synthesis, it is merely—if only briefly—to remind the reader that these pages are dedicated to one who knows well that such truths undergird all that he does. Metropolitan Philip— the young man who had the vision and hope to "dream the impossible dream," who has called his archdiocese to meet the new challenges of our age, who in the true Orthodox spirit of Antioch has aimed at always "incarnating" Christ anew in his efforts—knows that it is only because of that synthesis, albeit a paradox which "passes all understanding," that his many contributions have meaning.

CHAPTER 2

A SYNTHESIS OF
ECCLESIAL PERSPECTIVE

The Church began as a missionary movement. In the Apostolic Age, Antioch was the headquarters of the early missionaries such as Peter, Paul, and Barnabas. It is incumbent upon us, as children of Antioch, not only to keep the Faith and preserve it undefiled, but to spread the Faith and "make disciples of all nations."

Metropolitan Philip

Metropolitan Georges, one of the most prominent figures in the Patriarchate of Antioch, writes of a comprehensive synthesis, the ecclesial perspective, which captures the dynamic movement of the Church through her ecclesiology, anthropology, and sacramentology. He is aware of who God and man are, and how it is Christ who is the true mediator in our "coming together." Thus, the writer rightly comprehends the true theological context of our use of the term "synthesis," warning against an incorrect juxtaposition, for example, of Hegel and St. Maximus the Confessor. In this clear picture he is able to show that the final task of the Christian life is a theosis, a deification of humanity, in which our "salvation is perfected." This is only possible because our life is already "hid with Christ in God" (Col. 3:3).

J. J. A.

The Church in Movement

by

GEORGES KHODRE

The aim of this article is not to expound a theological theory, but to present a method, a way of looking at things. Therefore, there is no attempt here to elaborate a scientific, theological argument. Such an argument, no matter how sincere, always runs the risk of getting to the point of knowing how to inquire and not how to worship. Theology may perhaps be best communicated in the form of *doxology*, the type of insistent prayer that takes the Kingdom *by force* and establishes it among men (Matt. 11:12). Like Jacob at the brook of Jabbok, man is called to be an intercessor, a prince over the whole universe, who converses with God face to face, who "has power with God and with men and who prevails" in his fight for the transformation of life around him. In this process he is transformed, he becomes Israel, "he who strives with God," who has the power to transform the earth into "Peniel, the face of God" (Gen. 32:24-32).

As men wrestle with their situation in the context of what they know of God, He enlarges and deepens that knowledge. What we may need today is not another theological theory in which Christian "dialogue" takes the form of what Buber so rightly calls "a universal duel in the never-never-land of books,"[1] but the establishment of a person-to-person relationship, a passing from the realm of communication into that of *communion*.

[1] Martin Buber, *Between Man and Man* (London: Routledge & Kegan Paul, 1954) 34.

In this perspective, our first premise is the fact that biblical revelation points to and is based on endless situations of *human* existence in which God "speaks." The Jewish Torah is God's word to man. In the Old Testament God speaks. His word, will, and commandment are one: the creation of the whole universe as an expression of His own nature. As we move on to the New Testament, a second truth becomes clear to us: the Word, through whom all things were created at the beginning, God's speech to us, is *personal*. The life of Jesus, a human life in all the revealing human situations described and recorded in the Bible, is an integral part of God's revelation to man. God is Himself the *interpreter* of this history, as well as the *interpreted*. Thus, the Bible is not a mere historical account: it is "the cradle wherein Christ is laid," to use one of the favorite expressions of St. Ignatius of Antioch.[2] Since Christ, God's face, which had been obscured to man by sin, is turned toward the world, is appropriated, and finds its fulfillment in the human face. Having reestablished man's sunken image in its original dignity, the Word unites it to the divine beauty.

Furthermore, this process of appropriation, we would like to suggest, is a process that goes on in a human milieu, a communion of persons tied by a presence and called to be witnesses to this presence, to be the bearers of an awareness of the grace, love, fellowship, and joy of "God with us" (Matt. 1:23). This interpretation involves a person-to-person relationship. We cannot institutionalize the world into God's Kingdom, nor can we fulfill our ministry except by an intimate relationship with ordinary people. Seen in this perspective, the divine revelation in the Bible has to be expressed not merely as a historical and social element of the past, but rather as the incarnate Word in the Church. It is not simply a law to be followed, a set of facts to be believed, or even a history to be accepted. It is all this but it is also more: a relationship to be received and experienced (1 Cor. 2:12-16). This may be dismissed by some as being obscure mysticism. But there is in it something more than abstract emotionalism.

[2]*Epistle to the Church of Philadelphia*, quoted in Johannes Quasten, *Patrology* 1 (Utrecht: Spectrum Publishers, 1966) 73.

It is rather a Christ-mysticism, which, as such, is a "bound" mysticism—bound to history, to the event of the incarnation, which is being constantly renewed in the life of the Church and expressed in its inner life of prayer as a sacrifice of praise offered on behalf of the whole universe.

Our inquiry will then have three main dimensions: the *ecclesiological*, the *anthropological* and the *sacramental*. It is important for us to stress the fact that we do not intend here to present a discourse on the notion of the Church as "synthesis," either in the doctrines of the Church Fathers or in the works of other Christian theologians. We strongly believe that by doing so we would be forcing our own complex of ideas into the writings of the Fathers, who never intended to elaborate theological theories, but rather wrote out of the fulness of their hearts about the vision that was granted to them in their own life of prayer: "rooted and built up in Christ . . . abounding therein with thanksgiving . . . for in him dwelleth all the fulness of the Godhead bodily" (Col. 2:7-9). We will, therefore, purposefully refrain from engaging ourselves in any attempt at finding in the legacy of the Fathers any outline of a developed doctrine of the Church and its relationship to the world. Such an endeavor we believe would lead us to confusion as well as to obvious anachronisms like inserting Bergson into the work of St. Gregory of Nyssa or Hegel into the work of St. Maximus the Confessor. If we did this, our search would remain childless and barren like the daughter of the Egyptian king, in the words of St. Gregory of Nyssa:

> Childless, indeed, is pagan philosophy; always in pains of childbirth it never engenders living offspring. What fruit has philosophy brought forth worthy of such labor? Are not all [its fruits] inane and undeveloped and miscarried before they enter the light of the knowledge of God?[3]

---

[3]St. Gregory of Nyssa, *The Life of Moses* 2:11, quoted in Quasten 3:283-4.

The Ecclesiological Perspective

> Beloved, believe not every spirit, but try the spirits
> whether they are of God ... Every spirit that con-
> fesseth that Jesus Christ is come in the flesh is of
> God. ... Ye are of God, little children, and have over-
> come them, because greater is he that is in you, than
> he that is in the world. (1 John 4:1-4)

What the beloved disciple says here is that Christ has, in
fact, conquered the world. This victory consists in His having
created His own Church. He laid its foundations in the midst
of vanity and poverty, the weakness and suffering of human
history. The Church is the image and the abode of His blessed
presence in the world. He lives and abides ceaselessly in the
Church. In the Church we receive the spirit of adoption
through baptism (Rom. 8:15) and in it we are called to grow
to the full image of the stature of Christ. In the Church the
theosis of the human race is accomplished, and our salvation
is perfected. In it human life is, according to the words of
Paul, "hid with Christ in God" (Col. 3:3). Bishop
Theophanes explains the words of the Apostle by saying:

> Each one of us through baptism receives the fullness
> of Christ Jesus in the same manner as the good earth
> receives the grain in which the fullness of the tree is
> hid. All that is contained in the grain in a condensed
> manner, receives its full development in the tree.
> Through baptism our life is hid with Christ in God.
> It is only gradually through a painful process of growth
> that we enter into communion with him and that we
> attain to his fullness through the work of the Spirit in
> us.[4]

The Church is then completeness itself. Nothing lies out
of its realm as it encompasses human life in its entirety. It is
the continuation and the fulfillment of the incarnation, the

[4]From his commentary on Ephesians, cited in E. L. Mascall, ed., *The
Church of God* (London: SPCK, 1934) 55.

manifestation of Emmanuel, God-with-us. "Since the Incarnation of the Word," says St. Symeon the New Theologian, "everything is hid in the mystery of the human face of God."[5] The incarnation is the passing of man from darkness into light. Through it each one of us is placed under the vision of God. This is what our adoption as sons means. It is the sort of adoption that makes of each one of us a true partner with God as God "contemplates himself in us," according to the beautiful expression of St. Gregory Palamas.[6] We are called by the Father through the Son into a fellowship of love, the fellowship of the family of God, in which He always manifests Himself in a certain image, the image of God-in-us. He makes Himself clearly seen, we can fully recognize Him, He speaks to us and listens to us. We can see Him, touch the hem of His garment, and taste His goodness in every eucharistic service.

The community of the Church to which we are called is therefore transfigured and regenerated mankind. The meaning of this regeneration and transfiguration is that in the Church mankind becomes one unity, "in one body" (Eph. 2:16). The life of the Church is unity and union. The body is "knit together" and "increaseth in unity of Spirit, in unity of Love" (Col. 2:19).

The realm of the Church is *unity*, and of course, this unity is not an outward one but is inner, intimate, organic. It is the unity of the living body, the unity of the organism. In the Church humanity passes over into another plane, begins a new manner of existence. A new life becomes possible, a true, whole, and complete life, "in the unity of the Spirit, in the bond of peace" (Eph. 4:3). A new existence begins, a new principle of life, a life in the unity of Christ, "even as thou Father art in me and I in thee, that they also may be one" (John 17:21).

This is the mystery of the final reunion in the image of the Holy Trinity. And it is to this mystery, which Solovyev

[5]E. Kadloubovsky and G. E. H. Palmer, trs. and eds., *Writings from the Philokalia* (London: Faber & Faber, 1973) 143.

[6]E. Kadloubovsky and G. E. H. Palmer, trs. and eds., *Early Fathers from the Philokalia* (London: Faber & Faber, 1973) 409.

calls *sobornost*, i.e., the community of catholicity, that we are called.[7]

The catholicity of the Church denotes a unity of the Spirit, "in one spirit were we all baptized into one body" (1 Cor. 12:13). And the Holy Spirit, which is a Spirit of love and peace, not only unites isolated individuals, but also becomes in every separate soul the source of inner peace and wholeness. The catholicity of the Church means that the Church is a certain unity of life, a brotherhood or communion, a union of life, a life in common.

Perhaps this task of the Church as "gathering" the whole of the universe in Christ is best expressed in our Sunday Liturgy through the words of the priest who, after summoning us all to join with the celestial powers in a prayer of praise and thanksgiving, expresses our role as *intercessors* on behalf of the whole of creation which, through us, is brought into the presence of the Lord, so that it may be sanctified and regenerated—"Thine own of thine own we offer unto thee, on behalf of all and for all."

In his essay on the Virgin Mary, Bulgakov speaks of the Holy Virgin as the prototype of the Church, carrying the whole world in her prayer to the Father, through the Son, so that it would be regenerated by the fire of the Spirit blowing in its midst.[8] The whole universe is thus transformed through the Church's intercessory prayer into a burning bush, a source of light, burning with fire yet not consumed (Ex. 3:2):

> As deified she is in possession of all things. As the glory of God and the glory of the world, as the manifested love of God for the world and the manifested love of the world for God, in her prayer she glorifies God. Her own prayer is glorification, eternally realized love, flaming and triumphant in its perfect joy, God's own love for himself in his creation.[9]

[7]See Vladimir Solovyev, *The Justification of the Good*, tr. Nathalie A. Duddington (London, 1918) 199-298.

[8]S. Bulgakov, "The Burning Bush," in Nicolas Zernov, ed., *A Bulgakov Anthology* (London: SPCK, 1976) 90-6.

[9]Ibid., p. 95.

The Anthropological Perspective

In his commentary on Eph. 1:23, Origen speaks of the Church as the body of Christ "the fulness of him that filleth all in all." The Church is thus the manifestation of God's fulness, for it is the fulness of the creative Word, the divine "place" in which the whole of creation is gathered up in Christ.[10]

We come here to the very heart of Christian anthropology, as a key for a fuller understanding of the Church as synthesis. Perhaps this could best be expressed in Epiphanes' sermon on the baptism of our Lord, as he comments on 1 Cor. 15:45: "the first man Adam was made a living soul, the last Adam was made a quickening spirit." Through the Lord's baptism, he says, the second Adam descended to the lower parts of the earth (Eph. 4:9), in order to seek the first Adam lying there in captivity and to ascend with him up far above all the heavens, that He might fill all things:

> Adam lying in captivity spoke thus: "I hear footsteps approaching!" And as he spoke, the Lord entered carrying in his right hand the victorious weapon of the cross. Filled with awe Adam shouted to those in captivity: "My Lord be with you all!" and Christ answered saying, "And with your spirit . . . rise up from the dead. I am your God, and for your sake I have become your son . . . rise up and let us depart from here, for you are in me and I am in you, we both are one indivisible person. Rise up all of you and let us depart from the realm of pain to that of joy . . . the Kingdom which had been prepared for you from the beginning awaits you all."[11]

St. Maximus the Confessor elaborates on the mystery of God's image in man, fulfilled in Christ as the regenerated

[10]See Vladimir Lossky's article "The Theology of the Image," in his *In the Image and Likeness of God* (Crestwood, N.Y.: SVS Press, 1974) 125-39.

[11]PG 43:440, 464; cited in Leonid Ouspensky and Vladimir Lossky, *The Meaning of Icons* (Boston, 1969) 190.

Adam, by stressing the fact that in Christ the union between the divine *Fatherhood* and the earth's *motherhood* has been revealed. In Him the Father pulls human nature out of its own state of perdition. He delivers it from the state of estrangement into which it got itself, as it willed to be "like God," and restores it to its own dignity. In Christ, God's creative Word, in whom all things were made, recreated all things by achieving in Himself the restoration of man's sunken image. This He did by being fully human, but with a human will that realized its full manhood by being completely transparent to the will of the Father. Thus, the new creation in Christ is a reorientation of the whole process of nature through man, who was restored to his original role as co-creator with God.

Before the fall, Adam had the power of giving names to all created beings, of clothing them with their full reality, of extending the word to them (Gen. 2:19). But the fallen Adam no longer comprehended the lifegiving word that was in him; he chose to expel it out of his very being and preferred darkness to light. The old Adam was thus left to his own devices, which enabled him at best to see things "as though in a glass, darkly" (1 Cor. 13:12). The new Adam brought back to man the possibility of a full discernment. In Him man's vision was fully restored, for he was reestablished in his role as co-creator with God. With Christ the whole creation entered into a new reality, into a cosmic transfiguration, for it moved from the reality of God's sovereignty to that of His Fatherhood.[12]

St. Maximus then moves on to the Church as the human *receptacle* wherein God's Fatherhood is fully expressed. The Church is Christ's body in the sense that, in it, God's truth is fully acquired by the bond of baptism. The baptism of the Church is a baptism of fire (Matt. 3:11; Luke 3:16 and 12:49), which purifies and transfigures. In it the Spirit acts in man and through man, in free human love and sacrifice, not in power nor in the laws of nature, but as being placed under the law of the Spirit which vivifies. In the Church, the whole cosmos is restored to its own dignity, and each one of us is restored to his full dignity, for the Church as the body of Christ is the receptacle in which God gives Himself to the world and to us in Christ, through the Spirit, making out of the whole of creation a new mystery, the "cosmos of the cosmos." In this mystery, through us, the whole universe is gathered up in Christ Jesus.[13]

Thus, from the perspective of Christian anthropology, the Church is the heart of humanity. In this sense, humanity on its way to the fulness of Christ is the Church, seen in the mystery of God's Fatherhood. Likewise, the Church in its task of carrying in its inner life of prayer the whole of creation to the Father, is in itself Christ Jesus acting through the Spirit for the restoration of all things. In this sense, the Church holds in its bosom the salvation of the whole universe.

The Sacramental Perspective

Our inquiry into Christian anthropology has led us to the understanding of the Church as the holy place in which the whole of creation passes from death to life. To quote at length from the second theological oration of St. Gregory of Nazianzen (in which he explains the intercessory nature of the Church's task, as he speaks of the congregation at worship in terms of the people of Israel at Mount Sinai):

Now when I [as bishop] go up eagerly into the Mount—or to use a truer expression, when I both eagerly long, and at the same time am afraid (the one through my hope and the other through my weakness) to enter within the Cloud, and hold converse with God, for God so commands; if any be an Aaron [possibly referring to priests] let him go up with me, and let him stand near being ready, if it must be so, to remain outside the Cloud. But if any be a Nadad or an Abihu, or of the Order of the Elders [referring to

[13]Hans Urs Von Balthazar, *Liturgie Cosmique* (Paris: Aubier, 1947) 167-92.

the baptized], let him go up indeed, but let him stand
afar off, according to the value of his purification.
But if any be of the multitude [catechumens and un-
baptized], who are unworthy of this height of contemplation, if he be altogether impure let him not approach at all, for it would be dangerous to him; but
if he be at least temporarily purified, let him remain
below and listen to the Voice alone, and the trumpet,
the bare words of piety, and let him see the Mountain
smoking and lightning, a terror at once and a marvel
to those who cannot get up.[14]

Thus, according to St. Gregory, the Church is the *priest
of the world*. Through it God's voice is heard, His promise is
revealed. Should the multitude stand at the foot of the mountain in terror and marvel, the Church is called to stand on the
Holy Mountain, on behalf of the world, conscious of the
world's needs, interceding for it, in full identification with it,
not because it is wiser or holier but because God has called it
to know Him intimately, because each and every one in it
has put on Christ in baptism and has therefore been completely regenerated. This combination of access to the holy
presence and the holiness that develops in relation to that
access should characterize the life of the whole body of Christ.
This is their royal priesthood—to stand on behalf of the earth
before the King of kings, in High Priestly intercession and in
holiness of life. The act of worship is a moral act through
which we choose, on behalf of the whole world, the freedom,
beauty, truth, and perfection of God the Father through the
Son in the Holy Spirit. It is moral in the sense that it main-
tains us in the presence of the sacred humanity of our High
Priest (Heb. 9:11-12) in a surrendering silence.

In addition, then, to being of an intercessory nature, the
act of worship is also a time of "silence" before God. The
kind of silence we are talking about is, of course, not to be
understood as a mere cessation of speech. It is something
positive—an integral phenomenon of human life, like love

[14]Quoted in Paul Verghese, *The Joy of Freedom* (London: Lutterworth
Press, 1967) 68.

and death. It is not a pause between prayers, as though prayer is but noise. It is something without which words lose their meaning and turn into sounds made with the mere intention of being audible. Silence before God refers to an internal ascetic state of heart and mind through which others can "see the Mountain smoking and lightning, a terror at once and a marvel to those who cannot get up."

We are summoned to this silence during the Liturgy of Holy Saturday, as we sing in place of the Cherubimic hymn:

> Let all mortal flesh keep silence, and stand with fear and trembling; and let it take no thought for any earthly thing. For the King of kings and Lord of lords draws near to be sacrificed and given as food to the faithful.

This state of being present with God involves the sanctification of the whole universe. The whole Vesper service of Holy Saturday is imbued with this presence of the cosmic Christ sanctifying the whole of creation with the power of the cross. As the congregation sings the song of praise in the sixth tone, it joins the praise to God sung by the heavenly powers, by the clouds, the sun, the moon, the stars, light and darkness, rain, dew and winds, fire, snow, heat and cold, lightning and clouds, mountains, hills, and the whole of nature with all the creatures therein. At that moment of the Liturgy, the priest goes around the church throwing flowers and laurel leaves on the congregation, a symbol of the whole of creation gathered up into the Church's heart in a triumphant song of praise and joy.

We are also reminded of this state of being present with God at the ultimate hour at which we become one with the whole universe, every day throughout the year, during the midday prayers. At midday, at the sixth hour, the hour of the crucifixion, we join the praying Church as it lives each day anew, the hour at which God's love for us was made fully manifest on the cross of Calvary. After the trisagion prayer we sing: "O Christ our God, who at this hour didst stretch out Thy loving arms upon the cross that all men might be gathered unto Thee . . ."

St. Maximus the Confessor comments on the crucifixion by saying that it is the hour at which, on the internal scene of God's love, the whole cosmic drama between God and sin is displayed and comes to an end. It is the hour of the full redemption of the whole universe as the whole of creation is gathered up in God's heart. By the depth of His suffering, Christ becomes the blazing sun which "makes the world's crop mature and bear fruit, the fruit of unity." This is the great hidden mystery, the joyful end for which all was created. It was with His eyes set on this ultimate aim that God called forth the whole creation into existence.[15] St. Ignatius of Antioch goes on to say it is this love which cancels sin and abolishes death, the love of God's suffering servant, the truth of Christ's humanity, which he calls a "mystery of shouting accomplished in the silence of God."[16]

If we pass now with one leap from Ignatius of Antioch to John of Damascus, we hear him saying that God's love for the world is a passionate intensity, a freedom from restraint, which surmounts all barriers and holds nothing back. We are called to be co-workers with God as we participate in Christ's sacrifice through the Eucharist:

> Just as charcoal burns not of itself but through the fire with which it is impregnated.... I am but black cold charcoal. In order to be set ablaze by the fire of Pentecost, I want the bread of God, which is the flesh of Christ, of the seed of David, and I want to drink his blood, which is love incorruptible.[17]

This is the foundation stone of our royal priesthood. Being grounded in this love, we who are many become one, "that the Lord Jesus may be eaten through us by others and distributed to many," as we sing in the Vespers of the first Sunday in Lent. Through the eucharistic community the whole world is thus sanctified, purified, and transformed into the Kingdom.

[15]Von Balthazar, pp. 210-25.
[16]*Ephesians* 19:1; cited in G. L. Prestige, *Fathers and Heretics* (London: SPCK, 1977) 181.
[17]*De fide orthodoxe* 4:3; cited in Prestige, p. 183.

Conclusion: Transfiguration

What liturgical prayer tries to make us understand is the fact that there is no comprehensive perfection in a world full of fear, agony, and death. The litanies in our eucharistic Liturgy are full of petitions for peace for the whole world, for the welfare of the city and country to which we belong, for the sick, the suffering, for prisoners and captives. It thus expresses the Church's ardent struggle and striving for the transfiguration of man and of the world. The Liturgy points to the fact that the transfiguration of the world cannot be achieved through the mere setting up of a social structure, or through legal precepts and commandments which man does not have in his power to keep. It is principally and above all the result of God's taking upon Himself and transforming the sinful and decadent nature of man. This means that if a person believes in such a transfiguration, and thinks that it is worth pursuing for himself and his environment, it can be achieved only through faith in God who, by the incarnation and resurrection of Christ, makes such a thing attainable. In the Eastern Church, it is monks, not laymen, persons given to a life of prayer, who tried by their lives to preach the social ideals of the Church and thereby made up the ranks of its social army, which ministered to the needy and the oppressed.

This introduces into the prayer of the Church a moral dynamism of inestimable worth. Our communal choice to be on God's side influences the whole world. Through chrismation, we are anointed with a "priestly unction, a royal unction, a spiritual life-giving unction."[18] This unction is Christ's balm with which we are clothed. It is prepared out of forty-five kinds of natural balms and aromatic herbs cooked in oil and wine. Through it we are Christified, we put on Christ. Just as Christ's flesh is part of the created world,[19] our priestly office is also derived from the balms of the earth, so that, by assuming our royal calling, we can become co-workers with Christ in redeeming the whole of creation.

[18]Sung during the service of the preparation of the holy chrism.
[19]In the words of St. Athanasius; see Prestige, p. 182.

CHAPTER 3

THE SYNTHESIS OF
MAN AND REALITY

*A selfish man who cannot share,
who cannot give of himself, can
never experience the joy of the Eucharist. A man who separates himself from God's community can
never experience the true meaning
of membership in the Body of Christ,
which is the Church.*

Metropolitan Philip

Alexander Schmemann, Dean of St. Vladimir's Orthodox Theological Seminary, writes of the Eucharist as the sacrament of the Kingdom. Warning against an incorrect notion of the meaning of "symbol," he demonstrates that it is in a proper theological understanding of that word that the synthesis of man with God is realized. As one who has been the leading figure in the discipline of liturgical theology and has perhaps done more than anyone else to deepen the Orthodox consciousness of worship, Fr. Schmemann writes of the "two realities" of the Christian life in terms of "epiphany." In the context of the Eucharist as symbol and epiphany, then, the writer aptly reminds us that the Christian is a viator on the way to the experience of the Kingdom of God.

This article is to be incorporated into a forthcoming book on the Eucharist.

J. J. A.

The Symbol of the Kingdom

by

ALEXANDER SCHMEMANN

> "The time is fulfilled and the
> Kingdom of God is at hand."
> (Mark 1:15)

The Symbol as Presence and Reality

The expression "rich symbolism of Orthodox worship" is being used so frequently that for Orthodox and non-Orthodox alike it has become a familiar label, self-evident and requiring no further explanation—or rather this explanation is also taken for granted. Symbol is identified with "illustration," an act that *reminds us* of something else: an event of the past, an idea, a belief. Thus, it is said that the "little entrance" at the Divine Liturgy "symbolizes" the Savior's coming forth to preach the gospel, the "great entrance"—His burial, but also His solemn entrance into Jerusalem, etc. This "illustrative symbolism" has come to be applied to worship in general, whether taken as a whole or in each of its separate rites. And since this interpretation of "symbolism" (the flowering of which had begun already during the Byzantine period) is undoubtedly rooted in the most pious of feelings, it would occur to very few that not only does it not correspond to the basic and original conception of Christian worship, but actually distorts it and provides one of the reasons for its present decline.

In fact, "symbol" here designates something not only *distinct* from reality but in essence even *contrary* to it. For instance, the specifically western, Roman Catholic, emphasis upon the "real presence" of Christ in the eucharistic gifts grew out of a fear that this presence would be degraded into the category of the "symbolic." But this could only happen when the word "symbol" ceased to designate something *real* and became in fact the antithesis of reality. In other words, where one is concerned with "reality" there is no need for a symbol, and, conversely, where there is a symbol there is no reality. This led to the understanding of the liturgical symbol as an "illustration," necessary only to the extent that that which is represented is not "real." Thus, two thousand years ago the Savior came forth to preach the gospel in *reality*, and now we illustrate this act *symbolically* in order to recall for ourselves the meaning of the event, its significance for us, etc.

I repeat, these are pious and legitimate intentions in and of themselves. However, this type of symbolism is not only quite frequently utilized arbitrarily and artificially (thus the *entrance* at the Liturgy is turned into a symbol of Christ *coming out*), but in fact reduces ninety percent of our rites to the level of didactic dramatization. Such reduction deprives the rites of their inner necessity, their relation to the *reality* of worship. They become "symbolical" settings, mere decorations for the two or three acts or "moments" that alone provide, so to speak, "reality" to the Liturgy. This is demonstrated by our scholastic theology, which long ago in fact dismissed the entire *ordo* of the Eucharist from its field of interest and attention and concentrated entirely upon the isolated acts, the isolated "words of institution." On the other hand, it is also demonstrated (however strange it may seem) in our very piety. It is no accident, of course, that an increasing number of people in the Church find this piling up of symbolical representations and explanations disturbing to their prayer, distracting them from that spiritual reality, the direct contact with which is the very essence of prayer. The same "illustrative" symbolism that is unnecessary for the theologian is also unnecessary for the serious believer.

Therefore, it is extremely important that we emphasize that this "illustrative symbolism," which has gradually come to be virtually the only "key" to the explanation of worship, arose as a result of the collapse and decay of the *primary* understanding of the symbol. This collapse has had innumerable (and as yet not truly realized) consequences for Christianity as a whole. But, limiting ourselves to that which is truly germane to our topic, we will only say that this primary meaning of "symbol" is in no way equivalent to "illustration." In fact, it is possible for a symbol *not* to illustrate, i.e., it can be devoid of any external similarity with that which it symbolizes.

The history of religion shows us that the more ancient, the deeper, the more "organic" a symbol, the less it will be composed of such "illustrative" qualities. The reason for this is that the purpose and function of the symbol is *not* to illustrate (this would presume the *absence* of that which is illustrated), but rather to *manifest* and to *communicate* that which is symbolized. We might say that the symbol does not so much "resemble" the reality that it symbolizes as it *participates* in it, and is therefore capable of communicating with it in reality. In other words, the difference (and it is a radical one) between our contemporary understanding of the symbol and the original one consists in the fact that while today we understand the symbol as the representation (or sign) of an *absent* reality, in the original understanding it is the manifestation and presence of the *other* reality— which, under given circumstances, cannot be manifested and made present in any way other than as a symbol. This means that in the final analysis the true and original symbol is inseparable from faith, for faith is "the conviction of things unseen" (Heb. 11:1), the knowledge that there is another reality different from the "empirical" one and that it can be entered into, can be communicated with, can in truth become "the most real of realities."

Therefore, if the symbol presupposes faith, faith of necessity requires the symbol. For unlike "convictions," philosophical "points of view," etc., faith certainly is contact and a thirst for contact; embodiment and a thirst for embodiment:

it is the manifestation, the presence, the operation of one reality within the other. All of this *is* the symbol (from the Greek συμβάλλω, "unite," "hold together"). In it—unlike in a simple "illustration," simple sign, and even in the sacrament in its scholastic-rationalistic "reduction"—the empirical (or "visible") and the spiritual (or "invisible") are united not *logically* (this "stands for" that), nor *analogically* (this "illustrates" that), nor yet by *cause and effect* (this is the "means" or "generator" of that), but—to use a neologism— *epiphanically*. One reality *manifests* (from ἐπιφαίνω, "manifest") and *communicates* the other, but—and this is infinitely important—*only* to the degree to which the symbol itself is a "participant" in the spiritual reality and is able or called upon to embody it. In other words, in the symbol *everything* manifests the spiritual reality, but *not* everything pertaining to the spiritual reality appears embodied in the symbol. The symbol is always partial, always imperfect: "for our knowledge is imperfect and our prophecy is imperfect" (1 Cor. 13:9). By its very nature the symbol unites disproportionate realities, the relation of the one to the other always remaining "absolutely other." However *real* a symbol may be, however successfully it may communicate to us that other reality, its function is not to "quench" our thirst, but to intensify it: "Grant us that we may more perfectly partake of Thee in the never ending day of Thy Kingdom." It is not that this or that part of "this world"—space, time, or matter—be made *sacred*, but rather that everything in it be seen and comprehended as expectation and thirst for its complete spiritualization: "that God may be all in all" (1 Cor. 15:28).

Must we then demonstrate that only this ontological and "epiphanic" meaning of the word "symbol" is applicable to Christian worship? That we must raise our objections not against the undisputable symbolism of our liturgy but against that understanding and perception of the symbol in which it becomes a synonym for something "unreal," "not present," and against the explanation of "symbolism" as the antithesis of "realism"? That we reject "illustrative symbolism" not merely because it was unknown in the early Church (this would not in and of itself demonstrate its falseness), nor yet

because we prefer a different "key" (one, perhaps, more
relevant to our present psychology), but because in making
nominal almost the entire order of the Eucharist, in transforming it into a sequence of sacred dramatizations and alle-
gories, it thereby destroys the essence of genuine symbolism?

Now we can raise the basic question: what does the
Eucharist symbolize; what symbolism unites into a single whole
the entire *ordo* and all of its rites? Or, to put it differently,
what *spiritual reality* is manifested and given to us in this
"sacrament of all sacraments"?

The Eucharist as Revelation and Communion

The Liturgy begins with the solemn doxology: "Blessed
is the Kingdom of the Father, and of the Son, and of the
Holy Spirit, now and ever and unto ages of ages." The Savior
likewise began His ministry by proclaiming that the Kingdom
had come: "Jesus came into Galilee, preaching the gospel of
the Kingdom of God saying, the time is fulfilled and the
Kingdom of God is at hand: repent ye, and believe the
gospel..." (Mark 1:14-15). And it is with desire for the
Kingdom that the first and foremost of all Christian prayers
begins: "Thy Kingdom come."

Thus, the Kingdom of God is the content of the Christian faith—the goal, the meaning and the content of the
Christian life. It is the knowledge of God, love for Him, unity
with Him, and life in Him. The Kingdom of God is the unity
with God as the source of all life, indeed as life itself. It is
life eternal: "And this is eternal life, that they know Thee
the only true God..." (John 17:3). It is for this eternal life
in the fulness of love, unity, and knowledge that man was
created: "in Him was life and the life was the light of man"
(John 1:4). But man lost this in the fall, and by man's sin
evil, suffering, and death came to reign in the world. The
"prince of this world" came to reign; the world rejected its
God and King. But God did not reject the world. "He did
not cease to do all things until He had brought us up to
heaven, and had endowed us with His Kingdom which is to

come" (Anaphora of the Liturgy of St. John Chrysostom).
The prophets of the Old Testament hungered for this Kingdom, prayed for it, foretold it. It was the very goal and fulfillment toward which the whole sacred history of the Old
Testament was directed, a history holy not with human
sanctity (for it was utterly filled with falls, betrayals, and
sins) but with the holiness coming from its being God's
preparation for the coming of His Kingdom.

And now, "the time is fulfilled, and the Kingdom of God
is at hand" (Mark 1:15). The only-begotten Son of God became the Son of Man in order to proclaim and to give to
man forgiveness of sins, reconciliation with God, and new
life. By His death on the cross and His resurrection from the
dead He has come to reign. God "made Him sit at His right
hand in the heavenly places, far above all rule and authority
and power and dominion, and above every name that is
named . . . and He has put all things under His feet and has
made Him the head over all things" (Eph. 1:20-22). "Let all
the house of Israel therefore know assuredly that God has
made Him both Lord and Christ, this Jesus whom you crucified" (Acts 2:36). Christ reigns, and everyone who believes
in Him and is born again of water and the Spirit belongs to
His Kingdom and has Him within himself. "Christ is the
Lord." This is the most ancient Christian confession of faith,
and for three centuries the world, in the form of the Roman
empire, persecuted Christians who spoke these words for their
refusal to recognize *anyone* on earth as Lord except the One
Lord and One King.

The Kingdom of Christ is accepted by faith and is hidden
"within us." The King Himself came in the form of a servant
and reigned only through the cross. There are no external
signs of this Kingdom on earth. It is the Kingdom of "the
world to come," and thus only in the glory of His second
coming will all people recognize the true King of the world.
But for those who have believed in and accepted it, the Kingdom is already here and now, more obvious than any of the
"realities" surrounding us. "The Lord has come, the Lord is
coming, the Lord will come again. . ." This triune meaning
of the Aramaic exclamation "maranatha!" contains the whole

of the Christian's victorious faith, against which all persecutions have proven impotent.

At first glance all of this might sound like some sort of pious platitudes. But reread what we have just said and compare it with the faith and "experience" of the vast majority of Christians, and you will be convinced that the Kingdom of God has ceased to be the central content of and the inner motivation behind the Christian faith. Unlike the early Christians, those of later ages came, little by little, to lose the perception of the Kingdom of God as being "at hand." They came to understand it only as the Kingdom *to come*—at the end and *after* the end. "This world" and "the Kingdom," which in the Gospels are set side by side and in tension and struggle with one another, have come to be thought of in terms of a chronological sequence: now—only the world, then—only the Kingdom. For the first Christians the all-encompassing joy, the truly startling novelty of their faith lay in the fact that the Kingdom was *at hand*. It *had appeared*, and although it remained hidden and unseen for "this world," it was already present, its light had already shone, it was already at work in the world. Then, as the Kingdom was "removed" to the end of the world, to the mysterious and unfathomable reaches of time, Christians gradually lost their awareness of it as something hoped for, as the desired and joyous fulfillment of all hopes, of all desires, of life itself, of all that which the early Church implied in the words "Thy Kingdom come." It is characteristic that our scholarly and voluminous manuals of dogmatic theology (which cannot, of course, pass over the early doctrine in silence) speak of the Kingdom in quite sparing, dull, and even boring terms. Here, *eschatology* (i. e., the doctrine of the "final destiny of the world and man") is virtually reduced to the doctrine of "God as the Judge and Revenger." As to piety, i.e., the personal experience of individual believers, the interest is narrowed to the question of one's personal fate "after death." At the same time, "this world," about which St. Paul wrote that its form "is passing away" (1 Cor. 7:31), and which for the early Christians was transparent to the Kingdom, reacquired its own value and existence independent of the Kingdom of God.

This gradual narrowing, if not radical metamorphosis, of Christian eschatology, its peculiar break with the theme and experience of the Kingdom, has had tremendous significance in the development of liturgical consciousness in the Church. Returning to what we said above about the symbolism of Christian worship, we can now affirm that the Church's worship was born primarily as a *symbol of the Kingdom* and of the Church *as entrance into the Kingdom*. In "this world," the Church is the gift, the epiphany, and the anticipation of the Kingdom. The whole novelty, the uniqueness of the Christian cult was in its eschatological nature, as the presence here and now of the future, as the epiphany of that which is to come, as communion with the "world to come." As I wrote in my *Introduction to Liturgical Theology*,[1] it is precisely out of this eschatological experience that the "Lord's Day" was born as a *symbol*, i.e., the manifestation, now, of the Kingdom. It is this experience that determined the Christian "reception" of the Jewish feasts of Pascha and Pentecost, as feasts precisely of a "pass-over" from the present "aeon" to the one which is to come, and thus—symbols of the Kingdom of God.

But, of course, the symbol of the Kingdom par excellence, the one that fulfills all other symbols—the Lord's Day, baptism, Pascha, etc.—as well as the whole of the Christian life "hidden with Christ in God" (Col. 3:3), was the *Eucharist*— the sacrament of the coming of the risen Lord, of our meeting and communion with Him "at His table in His Kingdom" (Luke 22:30). Secretly, unseen by the world, "the doors being shut," the Church—that "little flock" to whom it was the "Father's good will to give . . . the Kingdom" (Luke 12:32)—fulfilled in the Eucharist her ascension and entrance into the light and joy and triumph of the Kingdom. And we can say, without any exaggeration, that it was from this totally unique and incomparable experience, from this fully *realized* symbol, that the whole of the Christian *lex orandi* was born

[1]Alexander Schmemann, *Introduction to Liturgical Theology* (London: Faith Press, 1966).

and developed. In terms used at the beginning of this chapter, we can say that, being the ultimate fulfillment of the symbol, the Eucharist, rather than "illustrating" anything, was the *revelation* of and the *communion* with everything.

The Orthodox Experience of the Kingdom

It should now be clear why it was that when the weakening and the eclipse of the original eschatology began, the liturgical symbolism of the Kingdom became overgrown little by little with the wild grass of secondary explanations and allegorical commentaries, i.e., with that "illustrative symbolism" which—as I tried to show above—in fact means the collapse of the symbol. As time went on, this original symbolism of the Kingdom came to be all the more forgotten. Inasmuch, however, as the liturgy, with its forms and its entire *ordo*, already existed and was perceived as an untouchable part of tradition, it naturally came to demand a new explanation—in conformity with the new "key." This was the beginning of an ever-deeper infiltration of "illustrative symbolism" into the explanation of worship.

The process, to be sure, was long and complicated and not some kind of instant "metamorphosis." One can also say that, whatever its external triumph, the "illustrative" symbolism has never completely succeeded in supplanting the original, eschatological symbolism of the liturgy. No matter how much development took place, for instance, in Byzantine worship in the direction of what, in my *Introduction to Liturgical Theology*, I termed "external solemnity," no matter how overgrown it became by decorative and allegorical details, by the pomp borrowed from the imperial cult and by terminology adopted from mysteriological "sacredness," worship as a whole as well as its deep intuition in the minds of the faithful continued to be determined by the symbolism of the Kingdom of God. And there is no better witness to this than the fundamental Orthodox *experience* of the temple and of iconography, an experience which crystalized precisely during the Byzantine period and in which the "holy of holies" of Orthodoxy is expressed better than in the repetitive rhetoric of the "symbolic" liturgical interpretations.

"Standing in the temple we stand in heaven." If, as we know today, the Christian temple developed primarily from the experience of the eucharistic gathering, it follows that also from the very beginning the idea of the temple implied the idea of *heaven on earth*, for the Eucharist is an ascension to heaven, our entrance into the heavenly sanctuary. This experience of the temple has survived almost unchanged and unweakened throughout the whole history of the Church, despite the numerous declines and breakdowns in the authentic traditions of church architecture and iconography. This experience constitutes that "whole" which unites and coordinates all the elements of the temple: space, form, shape, icons—all that which can be termed the *rhythm* and *order* of the temple. As to the icon, it is in its very essence a symbol of the Kingdom, the "epiphany" of the new creation, of heaven and earth full of God's glory, and it is for this reason that the canons forbid the introduction into iconography of any allegorical or illustrative "symbolism." For the icon does not "illustrate," it *manifests*, and does so only to the degree that it is itself a *participant* in what it manifests, inasmuch as it is both presence and communion. It is sufficient to have stood, be it only once, in the "temple of all temples," the Hagia Sophia in Constantinople—even in its present devastated and kenotic state—to *know* with one's whole being that the temple and the icon were born and nurtured in the living *experience of heaven*, in communion with the "joy and peace in the Holy Spirit" (Rom. 14:17), by which terms St. Paul defines the Kingdom of God.

This experience was frequently darkened. Historians of Christian art often speak of the decline of church architecture and the icon. And it is important to note that this decline usually came about by the *whole*—of the temple, of the icon—being weakened and lost beneath the thickening growth of details. Thus, the temple almost disappears under a thick layer of self-contained decorations, and in the icon, Byzantine as well as Russian, the original wholeness is replaced by an ever-growing attention to cleverly drawn details. Is this not the same movement—from the "whole" to the "particular," from the experience of the whole to a discursive "explanation," and, in short, from symbol to "symbolism"? And yet, as long as the "Christian world," the οἰκουμένη, born from the vision of Constantine, keeps, "relates" itself—be it imperfectly and sometimes nominally—to the Kingdom of God, the "longed-for homeland," this centrifugal movement cannot fully overpower the centripetal force. One might say that, at first and for a long period of time, the "illustrative" symbolism—be it in worship, in the icon, or in the temple— developed *inside* the initial and ontological symbolism of the Kingdom. The deeper and truly tragical break between the two of them, the initial replacement of the one by the other, began with the coming of the long (and in many ways continuing) "western captivity" of the Orthodox mind. It is not accidental that the luxuriant and unchecked flowering of "illustrative symbolism" corresponded in time with the triumph of western juridicism and rationalism in Orthodox theology, of pietism and sentimentality in iconography, of embellished "pretty" baroque in church architecture, of "lyricism" and emotionalism in church music. All of these manifest one and the same decline, one and the same "pseudomorphosis" of the Orthodox consciousness.

Yet even this deep and truly tragical decline cannot be considered final. In its depths, the Church's consciousness ultimately remains untouched by all of this. Thus, everyday experience shows us that "illustrative symbolism" is foreign to the living, authentic faith and life of the Church, just as "scholastic" theology remains foreign, in the last analysis, to such faith. "Illustrative symbolism" is at home in that superficial, "showy," and routine churchliness in which a widespread but shallow curiosity toward all sorts of "symbolism" is lightly taken as religious feeling and "interest in the Church." But where there is a living, authentic and (in the best sense of the word) *simple* faith, it becomes *unnecessary*, for genuine faith lives not by curiosity but by thirst.

Just as he did a thousand years ago, so today the "simple" believer goes to church in order primarily to "touch other worlds" (Dostoevsky). In a sense, he is not "interested" in worship, in the way in which "experts" and connoisseurs of all liturgical details are interested in it. And he is not interested because "standing in the temple" he receives all that for which he thirsts and seeks: the light, the joy, and the comfort of the Kingdom of God, that *radiance* which, in the words of the agnostic Chekhov, beams from the faces of the "old people who have just returned from the church." What use could such a believer have for complex and refined explanations of what this or that rite "represents," of what the opening or closing of the royal doors is supposed to mean? He cannot keep up with all these "symbolisms," and they are unnecessary for his faith. All he knows is that he has left his everyday life and has come to a place where everything is *different* and yet so essential, so desirable, so vital that it illumines and gives meaning to his entire life. Likewise he knows that this *other* reality makes life itself worth living, for everything proceeds to it, everything is related to it, everything is to be judged by it—by the Kingdom of God it manifests. And, finally, he knows that even if individual words or rites are unclear to him, the Kingdom of God has been given to him in the *Church*: in that common action, common standing before God, in love and unity.

Conclusion

Thus we return to where we began, indeed to where the Eucharist itself begins: to the blessing of the Kingdom of God, as its content and all-encompassing meaning. What does it mean to *bless* the Kingdom? It means that we acknowledge and confess it to be our highest and ultimate value, the object of our desire, our love, and our hope. It means that we proclaim it to be the goal of that *sacrament*—of pilgrimage, ascension, and entrance—which now begins. It means that we must focus our attention, our mind, heart, and soul, i.e., our whole life, upon that which is truly "the one thing needful." Finally, it means that now, already in "this world," we confirm the possibility of communion with the Kingdom, of entrance into its radiance, truth, and joy. Each time that

Christians gather in the church they witness before the whole world that Christ is King and Lord, that His Kingdom has already been revealed and given to man and that a new and immortal life has begun. This is why the Liturgy begins with this solemn confession and doxology of the King who comes *now* but abides forever and shall reign unto ages of ages.

Amen, answer the people. This word is usually translated as "so be it," but its meaning is really stronger than this. It signifies not only agreement, but also active acceptance: "Yes, this is so, and *let* it be so." With this word the ecclesial assembly concludes and, as it were, *seals* each prayer uttered by the celebrant, thereby expressing its own organic, responsible, and conscious participation in each and every sacred action of the Church. "To that which you are—say Amen," writes St. Augustine, "and thus seal it with your answer. For you hear 'the Body of Christ' and answer Amen. *Be* a member of the Body of Christ, which is realized by your Amen . . . Fulfill that which you are."

CHAPTER **4**

THE SYNTHESIS OF
FAITH AND ETHICS

> *The past is history. History becomes meaningful when time is dedicated to the fulfillment of God's purpose.*
>
> Metropolitan Philip

Everyone who has heard the name of John Meyendorff associates it with Byzantine Christian history. In this chapter, however, Fr. Meyendorff treats the reader to a lesson in "history," but not in the usual sense of that word. As any historian would, he does deal with time, but now with that time upon which all Christian time is based: the triduum, the time from Holy Friday through Holy Saturday to the blessed Pascha. He attempts to deal with the theological question of what happened in the time between Friday and Sunday, the time of Christ's redemptive work in His sojourn in the tomb. Using liturgical and hymnographical sources to establish Orthodox theological presuppositions, the writer takes the reader on an uncommon journey to the point where Holy Saturday serves as the juncture where faith and ethics are synthesized. Thus, the renowned Orthodox historian establishes what he calls the "ethics of the resurrection."

J. J. A.

The Time of Holy Saturday

by

JOHN MEYENDORFF

A full and proper understanding of the mystery of the Christian faith inevitably implies a *time* dimension. It often seems that one of the reasons why contemporary Christianity—and contemporary Orthodoxy—loses sight of the reality of human life is that it attempts to preach only abstract and "timeless" ideas about faith and ethics. But biblical revelation, unlike philosophical systems, is not limited to eternal ideas. It is a revelation of facts, actions of God in history—the act of creation, the act of the election of Abraham and his descendants, the act of leading Israel out of slavery, and, finally, the act of the incarnation. The incarnation itself is a story, a continuum, a process. In becoming man, the Son of God does not assume an abstract humanity, but becomes a human individual, Jesus of Nazareth, who was born as a child, "grew in wisdom and stature," and lived to maturity in human life. Eventually, He met with the hostility of various religious and political groups in the society in which He lived, was crucified and died on the cross, but rose from the dead on the third day. His death and resurrection—the facts that constitute the very foundation of the Christian faith—were events occurring *in time*.

We cannot perceive the full meaning of the Christian kerygma without meditating on what was happening between the ninth hour on Holy Friday and the early hours of the paschal Sunday. No theology of redemption will ever be complete or adequate if it considers the death of Christ and

His resurrection as two momentary and separate events. The real significance of the paschal mystery is revealed in the liturgical *triduum*—a "mystery" itself, which manifests the fulness of Christ's humanity as well as the entire dimension of divine love. Neither of these aspects of redemption could be adequately shown without the *time* element, for man lives and dies in time, and it is this concrete human life that God came to assume and redeem.

Thus, the climax of the redemptive ministry of Jesus Christ coincides with His sojourn in the grave: the mystery of Holy Saturday. Liturgical drama expresses this mystery much better than conceptual propositions. The liturgy, however, is based on a kerygma, expressed in theological terms. And therefore we shall first look at some theological presuppositions, and then at Holy Saturday itself, in its Byzantine liturgical expression.

Theological Presuppositions: "God suffered in the flesh"

The liturgical and hymnographical developments that entered into the structure of the offices of Holy Week in Byzantium are intimately connected with the fundamental Christological positions taken at the councils of Nicea (325), Ephesus (431), Chalcedon (451), and Constantinople (553). These councils affirmed the divine identity of Jesus as the incarnate Logos, consubstantial with the Father. The great Alexandrian tendency in Christology, represented by St. Cyril in his struggle against Nestorius, insisted particularly on the fact that *God Himself*—not some created intermediary—was the agent of salvation. No one else but the Son of God could be the *Savior* of creation, because He was also its Creator, as well as the Prototype, whose image had been bestowed upon man.

The issue between Cyril and Nestorius was the question of whether the *same* incarnate Logos could be both God and also fully man. Antiochian Christology was reluctant to admit that God himself—changeless and immortal in His *nature*—could be *born* of Mary and *die* on the cross. For the Antiochians, such essentially human events could only happen to a distinct human individual: the son of Mary. Immutability and immortality were divine attributes from which God could not depart. In Jesus, therefore, God and man remained not only distinct, but also somehow separated by the essential characteristics of their respective natures. Jesus' identity was inevitably dual, even to the point of making it *uncertain* whether it was possible or not to address Him as a *single person.*

In its extreme form, this tendency of thought resulted in Nestorianism. But the unity of Christ, as the preeternal Son of God, was then reaffirmed by the councils, which, however, also maintained the full integrity of His human nature. His human birth and human death were possible only because He was fully man. The main intention of St. Cyril of Alexandria was to preserve the identity of Christ as the *Savior.* God alone can *save,* because He "alone has immortality" (1 Tim. 6:16). While being God, He brought Himself not only to humanity itself, but to the very depths of human degradation, the ultimate degree of fallenness—death itself. For St. Cyril, salvation came precisely from the fact that "one of the Holy Trinity suffered in the flesh." This Cyrillian "theopaschism" was rationally unacceptable to the Nestorianizing theologians (as it still is to many of their modern followers), because for them God remains a prisoner of philosophical concepts that determine His "nature"—God simply cannot be "born" of Mary, and certainly cannot "die." Therefore, some other person was the subject involved in that birth (Mary was only the mother of a man, Jesus) and in that death. These, however, are philosophical objections to realities that transcend philosophy. The ultimate and unfathomable love of the personal triune God for His creation and His will to *be* where fallen humanity was—in death itself—in order to *save* it, cannot be expressed in terms of "human wisdom."

In order to better realize the true dimensions of this patristic "death of God" theology of St. Cyril, one must also remember that human mortality, voluntarily assumed by the incarnate Logos, was both the consequence and, in a sense, the cause of human sin. Death and sin are inseparable cosmic realities in fallen creation, because "through one man sin entered into the world, and through sin death, and thus death passed unto all men" (Rom. 5:12). According to the prevailing patristic exegesis of that passage, then, it is this universal mortality that makes personal sinfulness inevitable. Dominated by suffering, fear of death, and insecurity, man came under the power of an instinct for *self*-protection and *self*-preservation. He began to struggle for his *own* survival, at the expense of his neighbor, even if this survival could be only temporary (and therefore illusory), since "death reigned from Adam to Moses, even upon those who did not sin as Adam did" (Rom. 5:14). Indeed, it still reigns, in spite of all human efforts to conquer it, except by Jesus, the Christ.

Mortality is, therefore, the ultimate condition of fallen man. It keeps him enslaved, dependent, and inevitably concerned about his threatened self, with a tendency to use others for his own selfish interests.

The vicious circle of death and sin, however, was *broken* by God Himself, who came "to serve, and not to be served," who said that it is "better to give, than to receive," and "who gave Himself for the salvation of many." In a world where struggle for survival at the expense of others is the law, He showed that death for others is the ultimate act of love. And when this act was performed by God Himself, a new life indeed came into the world.

This "redemption" brought by Christ defies rational explanation, yet its significance is overwhelming. It is an event that took place in history, that, like all historical events, took time: the time of Jesus' earthly life, and the three days of His burial.

The Liturgical Expression: The New Passover

In the *lex orandi* of the early Church—which is still preserved in many ways in the Byzantine liturgical tradition—the two main parts of the daily office are connected, respectively, with the gradual coming of daylight in the morning and sunset in the evening. In both cases, the structure of liturgical prayer is eschatological. In addition to commemorating an already *given* event, it is always a "building up," it is oriented toward *forthcoming* events. The purpose is to create a sense of expectation: the morning light, the sign of the risen and saving Christ, is being expected and eventually met. In actual parish practice—which has become quite detached from the cycles of nature—this general daily pattern may not always be obvious, but without it the development and meaning of the liturgy remains incomprehensible.

One must also bear in mind that the Byzantine liturgical day—following Jewish tradition—begins in the evening, or, more precisely, in the very middle of the office of Vespers (at the prokeimenon). Consequently, the mystery of Holy Saturday starts on the afternoon of Holy Friday. The office of Vespers for Holy Friday—beginning at the ninth hour, i.e., 3:00 p.m., the very time that Jesus died on the cross— also inaugurates the "Great Sabbath."

Expressed with great drama and tragedy, the apparent victory of evil and death finds its fulfillment in the prokeimenon of Vespers:

Thou hast put me in the depths of the Pit, in the
regions dark and deep. (Ps. 88:6)
Verse: O Lord, the God of my salvation: I call for
help by day, I cry out in the night before Thee!

The prokeimenon is followed by the reading of 1 Corinthians 1:18-2:2 ("I decided to know nothing among you except Jesus Christ and Him crucified") and a long selection of passion narratives from Matthew, Luke, and John.

As soon as these readings are completed, however, the hymns suddenly become triumphant in tone:

Hell shuddered when it beheld Thee,
The Redeemer of all who was laid in a tomb.
Its bonds were broken; its gates were smashed!
Its tombs were opened; the dead arose.
Then Adam cried in joy and thanksgiving:
Glory to Thy condescension, O Lover of man!

This triumph in death expresses the basic position of Cyrillian Orthodox Christology: here is the burial of Jesus, but in effect, it is the Son of God Himself who is being buried in order to destroy the power of death *from within*:

> Being boundless and infinite by nature of Divinity,
> Thou wast bound and enclosed in a tomb by nature
>   of the flesh.
> Thou didst close the chambers of death and hell;
> Thou didst empty all of their kingdoms, O Christ!
> This Sabbath Thou also didst make worthy
> Of Thy blessing, glory, and splendor.

In contemporary practice (both Greek and Slavic), the real meaning of the evening services on Holy Friday has become somewhat overshadowed by more rudimentary—and certainly more recent—expressions of emotional piety. For example, in the Russian practice, Vespers of Holy Friday ends with a solemn procession of the epitaphion (Slavic: *plashchanitsa*, "shroud") to the middle of the church, where it is offered for the veneration of the faithful. The epitaphion is an iconographic image of the dead Christ, and the procession is understood as a symbolic reenactment of Christ's burial. Similar associations with Christ's burial are commonly suggested for the Matins service, celebrated in the late evening of Holy Friday, which we will discuss later. The hymns, it is true, do contain references to Joseph of Arimathea, Nicodemus, and the myrrhbearing women, but the service as a whole is much more than simply another funeral procession, or a means to evoke sorrow and lamentation. In actual fact, Byzantine art did not know any image of the *dead* Christ before the eleventh century, and the now popular epitaphion image is essentially an imitation of the sixteenth-century Italian *pietà*. Still, even in reducing the meaning of Holy Friday to a commemoration of Christ's burial, popular piety did not eliminate the *triumph* underlying the sorrow, which is so explicit in the liturgical texts.

The troparia sung at the end of Vespers combine the theme of Joseph of Arimathea's devoted mourning with an anticipation of the announcement of the resurrection:

The noble Joseph, when he had taken down
Thy most pure body from the tree, wrapped it
In fine linen and anointed it with spices,
And placed it in a new tomb.

The Angel came to the myrrhbearing women at the
    tomb
And said: "Myrrh is meet for the dead,
But Christ has shown Himself a stranger to corrup-
    tion."

The death of Christ is already a victory. It is impossible to
commemorate it only by mourning, because it is *God Himself*
who joined the dead and shared *our* condition of mortality.
The dead are no longer alone in the tomb! Triumph is forthcoming! The Church knows this and cannot act as if darkness had really overcome light, as it seemed to those who did
not believe in the divine identity of Jesus. Hence, the paradoxical combination of sorrow and joy that permeates the
liturgy on Holy Saturday.

The office of Matins for Holy Saturday—usually celebrated later in Friday evening and popularly called the
"Lamentations"—represents a development of the same subdued yet gradually more explicitly triumphant theme. Framed
in the *usual* structure of Byzantine Matins, the proper order
of this Matins service conveys a particularly triumphant theme
in three characteristic elements: Psalm 119, the canon, and
the procession.

In place of the usual chanting of the regular psalms at
Matins, which is done while sitting (*kathismata*), this service calls for the recitation of the one long Psalm 119, a poetic
praise of the Law known as the *Amomon* (from its beginning in Greek). The psalm is divided into three sections,
called *staseis*, which indicate that the chanting was done in
a *standing* position. A hymn characteristic of late pre-Chris-
tian Judaism, Psalm 119 praises the Law as the ultimate delight, a source of refreshment and joy. In the liturgy of Holy
Saturday, the psalm obviously points to Jesus, who fulfilled
the Law in His death. Accompanying each of the 176 verses

of the psalm are short "praises" (ἐγκώμια—wrongly termed
"lamentations") of the victory of Christ over death, composed by an unknown Greek poet of the post-Byzantine period.
The author of these "praises" had a very keen sense of the
mystery, pointing briefly to various aspects of emotional
and/or theological significance, and always aware of the fact
that the victory over death is *already* won:

> Thee do we magnify, O Jesus King. We honor Thy
> Passion and Thy burial, through which Thou hast
> delivered us out of corruption.

> Though hidden in a tomb, O Christ, Thou wast not
> separated from the Father's bosom. Verily, it is a
> strange matter, exceedingly wonderful.

> In a new tomb Thou wast placed, O Christ, renew-
> ing the nature of mankind, when Thou didst rise
> from the dead, as God.

Toward the end of the *staseis*, the rhythm accelerates into
briefer exclamations, as if the poet was becoming impatient
with Christ still lying in the tomb:

> A dread and strange sight, O Word, that the earth
> doth hide Thee.

> The women with spices come early at dawn to the
> tomb to anoint Thee.

> By Thy Resurrection grant peace to the Church and
> salvation to Thy people.

And, addressing Mary, the Mother of God:

> Grant your servants, O blessed Theotokos, to behold
> the Resurrection of your Son.

Finally, as a response to the singing of the psalm and the

praises, comes the triumphant resurrection hymn, sung at the eulogetaria of Matins every Sunday:

The angelic host was filled with awe when it saw Thee among the dead. By destroying the power of death, O Savior, Thou didst raise Adam and save all men from hell.

The Myrrhbearers were sorrowful as they neared Thy tomb. But the angel said to them, "Why do you number the living among the dead? Since He is God, He is risen from the tomb."

The second characteristic element of Matins of Holy Saturday is the entire body of hymnography comprising the canon of Matins and the verses of the praises, sung at Saturday evening Vespers. The Greek poetic forms of the hymns are not always easy to translate, but their theological content has nourished generations of Orthodox Christians in many languages. The theme is still that of a subdued triumph over death. Here is Christ Himself addressing His mother:

Lament not for Me, O Mother,
When you see me in the grave—your Son, whom you conceived virginally.
For, as God, I shall rise and shall be glorified,
And lift up in glory those who with faith and love magnify you.

Another theme constantly recurring in the hymns is Christ's descent into Hades. This is not simply a symbolic image—it affirms that Christ shares the fate of fallen mankind as a whole, in order to return it to life by His presence in its midst. One should also remember that in Scripture and in Greek patristic literature death and Hades (or "hell") are perceived as personalized—e.g., "death reigned from Adam to Moses" (Rom. 5:14). In other words, we have here another designation of Satan himself, the "usurper," the "murderer from the beginning," who holds the entire cosmos in captivity. In the Holy Saturday hymns, Hades itself speaks:

Today, Hell cries out groaning:
"My dominion has been shattered.
I received a dead man as one of the dead,
But against Him, I could not prevail.
From eternity I had ruled the dead,
But behold, He raises all.
Because of Him do I perish."
Glory to Thy cross and resurrection, O Lord.

Today, Hell cries out groaning:
"My power has been trampled upon.
The Shepherd is crucified and Adam is raised.
I have been deprived of those whom I ruled.
Those whom I swallowed in my strength, I have given
    up.
He who was crucified emptied the tombs.
The power of death has been vanquished."
Glory to Thy cross and resurrection, O Lord.

The tomb of Christ is a cause of bitterness and dismay for
the powers of death and evil, not for liberated mankind. For
us, on the contrary, it is the accomplishment of a new creation through the resurrection. Holy Saturday, then, parallels
the seventh day, when God rested in satisfaction with His
creation.

The great Moses mystically foreshadowed this day,
    when he said:
"God blessed the seventh day."
This is the blessed Sabbath.
This is the day of rest,
On which the only-begotten Son of God
Rested from all His works.
He kept the Sabbath in the flesh
Through the dispensation of death.
But on this day, He returned again through the resur-
    rection,
And has granted us eternal life,
For He alone is good, the lover of man.

We now turn to the third characteristic element of the celebration of Holy Saturday. In the present practice, Holy Saturday Matins continues with a procession around the church with the "shroud" or "tomb" of Christ. This procession symbolically includes the whole cosmos in the mystery of Christ's death and resurrection, for the mystery pertains not only to the personal, individual survival of faithful human beings, but also to the transfiguration of the entire creation.

When the procession returns to the nave of the church, the triumph over death is celebrated with the reading of Ezekiel's vision of the dry bones in the valley (37:1-15). This reading, at least in some areas, has become very popular and is chanted with great solemnity.

The next two readings are from the New Testament, accompanied by liturgical expressions of hope and joy from the Old Testament. The mood of expectation is heightened by the prokeimenon: "Arise, O Lord, my God; let thy hand be lifted up; do not forget thy poor forever" (Ps. 74). The epistle itself, drawn from Galatians, points to the resurrection ("a little leaven leaveneth the whole lump"—Gal. 5:9). Then, in anticipation of the paschal Vigil service, the alleluiarion proclaims "Let God arise, and let His enemies be scattered" (Ps. 68:1), while the Gospel returns to the historical account of Christ's entombment in Matthew 26: the soldiers "went and made the sepulchre sure, sealing the stone and setting a watch."

In the evening of Holy Saturday the paschal Vigil begins. However, the first and major part of the Vigil—Vespers and the baptismal Liturgy of St. Basil—are frequently celebrated on Saturday morning, because in the early Church, baptism, being the new birth in Christ, was always bestowed upon catechumens on that day.

Conclusion: A Realized Eschatology

We have noted at the beginning of this article that, in Greek patristic tradition, mortality and death—rather than inherited guilt—mark the essential reality of the fallen world.

Consequently, the death of Christ is contemplated not so much in terms of resolving a judicial contest or restoring peace between contending parties, nor as a satisfaction of divine justice. Rather, redemption is understood as a dramatic and violent intrusion of God into the realm where Satan held sway. Satan then perishes, for he cannot hold God prisoner. In describing redemption, St. Gregory of Nyssa, one of the great Cappadocian fathers of the fourth century, used the image of a fisherman's rod: Satan "swallowed" what he saw as nothing more than another helpless human being, but was "hooked" by the overwhelming presence of God Himself. The same idea appears in the homily attributed to St. John Chrysostom, which has become an integral part of the paschal Vigil:

> Let no one be fearful of death, for the death of the Savior has set us free. He has quenched it by being subdued by it. He who came into Hades, despoiled Hades . . . Hades received a body, and encountered God. It received mortal dust, and met Heaven face to face . . . O Death, where is your sting? O Hades, where is your victory?

The liturgy does not fail to recall the tragedy, the ugliness, the humiliation of Christ's death: His trial, the betrayal, the human weakness. But it also refuses to accept an artificial and emotional contrast between Holy Friday and Easter—it is at the very moment of Christ's death that His ultimate power over death is recognized. This is why the tragedy of *every human death* can be overcome by the fact that Christ has also shared it on Holy Saturday.

Man's fallen condition makes his struggle for a limited and temporary survival inevitable. Also quite inevitably, this struggle is at the expense of the neighbor, of the weak, and of nature itself, which God had created so that it could be put to better use. Man cannot stop being concerned with his food, his clothing, his health, his physical security, even if his concern hurts others and even if he knows that his survival can only be temporary. Yet the resurrection of Jesus Christ—

an event that did happen in time—makes Christian hope possible.

How is it possible not to be anxious about one's life, what one shall eat or what one shall drink, what one shall put on? (cf. Matt. 6:25) Is it really possible for man to live "like the lilies of the field"? Is not the Sermon on the Mount nothing but unrealistic sentimentalism? Indeed it is, if it is not seen in the light of the *ethics of the resurrection*. In Christ, death has been vanquished, and thus the basis for fear and for the perennial struggle for survival has also disappeared. The law of the fallen world, based on self-defense, self-affirmation, and demands pressed upon others, has been suppressed. The New Testament affirms that it is "better to give, than to receive"—unconditionally.

Holy Saturday is a proclamation of "realized eschatology." The end, the goal of creation, where "death shall be no more" (Rev. 21:4) is made accessible to human freedom, to faith, and to immediate human experience. The Passage, the Passover, the Pascha, has begun!

CHAPTER 5

A SYNTHESIS OF CHRISTIAN VIEW AND INDIVIDUAL RESPONSE

> *Very often people ask me, "What can I do to become religious?" This is a common question in a push-button and technological culture. We don't have pills which can make us religious. Read the Scripture; study the Lives of the Saints; give yourself to the sacramental life of the Church; then God will illumine your heart and show you the way.*
>
> Metropolitan Philip

Stanley Harakas, who served as Dean of Holy Cross Greek Orthodox School of Theology for ten years while also teaching Orthodox Christian ethics, is one person who has always brought the faith to bear on the questions of the day. When others have circumvented some of these issues, Fr. Harakas has spoken out. In this chapter he takes up the delicate issue of the morality of war, presenting the reader a synthesis of the Christian view and the individual response. After taking the reader through various moral and political dimensions of war and a critique of the three classic responses, he then presents the alternatives available to the individual Christian on the solid basis of Orthodox ethics. Here is a creative Orthodox Christian response to an eternal and ever-increasing danger to humankind: war.

J. J. A.

The Morality of War

by

STANLEY HARAKAS

> "The gentlest man cannot live in
> peace, if it does not please his
> wicked neighbor."
>
> (Schiller, *William Tell*)

Relating the Orthodox Christian faith to the realities of
life is not always the most congenial activity for us, even
though we consistently deny that Orthodoxy is a system of
teaching or an objective, rational approach, affirming to the
contrary that Orthodoxy is a "way of life." One of the most
difficult and problematic issues in relating the Orthodox faith
to concrete realities is the issue of war. As we shall see below,
this does not mean that an ethical teaching of the Orthodox
Church about war is lacking. However, the very nature of
that teaching has tended to deal with the moral issue of war
in broad and general terms, i.e., as a phenomenon on broad
levels of theory, national interests, patriotism, etc. Moreover,
the issue took on a different and more complex dimension
during the Vietnam War debates of the late sixties and early
seventies.[1] The topic of individual response to the call of the

[1]See, for example, the June 7, 1968 policy statement of the National
Council of Churches of Christ, "Religious Obedience and Civil Disobedi-
ence"; William Sloan Coffin, Jr., "On Civil Disobedience," *Una Sancta*
(Pentecost 1967) 27-33; Abe Fortas, *Concerning Dissent and Civil
Disobedience* (New York: New American Library, 1968); Alan Geyer,
"The Just War and the Selective Objector," *Christian Century* (Feb. 16,

nation to serve in the armed forces took on a new dimension: it was no longer presented as an avoidance of one's duty to the common defense. Rather, the assumption that the individual could and should make moral judgments about the rightness or wrongness of a particular war came to be accepted as a matter of course. It was not traditional pacifism, as exemplified in the slogan "What if they gave a war and no one came?" The issue raised was whether the individual citizen had the moral responsibility to *subjectively* determine if a particular military action was moral or not, and then to determine whether he or she should serve or refuse to serve. The Supreme Court of the United States denied legality to the issue, but the moral issue persists.

With the end of the war in Vietnam, as well as the end of the draft in the United States and the establishment of an all-volunteer army, the importance of the issue seemed to have died, despite continued concern for the possibility of a nuclear holocaust.[2] However, recent international events have served to awaken concern with the question of war in general. President Carter's call for registration in anticipation of a draft has sharpened the issue and calls all of us, especially young people, to respond once again. This presentation is an effort to address the issue out of the tradition of the Eastern Orthodox Church. It is timely that we do it now, during peace, when some measure of calm will allow a certain measure of discussion and searching for a clarification of an Orthodox position on the issue.

A good example of the need for this is to be found in Daniel Poling's introduction to his book *A Preacher Looks at War*.[3] Poling, who in his time was a well-known clergyman,

1966); Robert F. Drinan, *Democracy, Dissent and Disorder* (New York: Seabury, 1969); Daniel B. Stevick, *Civil Disobedience and the Christian* (New York: Seabury, 1968); Gordon C. Zahn, *War, Conscience and Dissent* (New York: Hawthorne Books, 1967).

[2]See Robert McAfee Brown, "Modern Warfare: Notes for Christian Reflection," *Christianity and Crisis* (May 14, 1973); Paul T. Jersild and Dale A. Johnson, eds., *Moral Issues and Christian Response*, 2d ed. (New York: Holt, Rinehart and Winston, 1976) 267-74; Sylvester P. Theisen, "Man and Nuclear Weapons," *The American Benefictive Review* (Sept. 1963).

[3]Daniel Poling, *A Preacher Looks at War* (New York: Macmillan, 1943).

author, and editor, describes an illuminating personal experience. Between the First and Second World Wars, America went through a period of widespread pacifism, related, of course, to the political isolationalism dominant at that time. During that period, a group of clergymen, to which Poling belonged, took a public position espousing pacifism. Poling was the only member of the group who refused to go along. Later, he had the opportunity to take an "I told you so" attitude when the United States entered the war against the Axis powers and all the former pacifist clergymen of the group changed their views and became advocates of the rightness of the war against the Fascists and the Nazis.

In a certain sense this reflects the simple fact that when Christians think about the Christian view of war they are highly influenced in their thoughts by the political exigencies and realities of the time and place in which they live and think. This, of course, is inevitable; we often do our thinking this way. But if we want to think about the institution of war and our Christian commitment as fairly stable phenomena, then it is necessary to do some deeper thinking and to be on a level of thought that is more inclusive than one that simply responds to the politico-socio-economic and polemic situations in which we find ourselves from time to time. So, even though it is my concern to direct myself to the question of the individual's response to the question of war, very little of significance can be said if at least some factors of more enduring, general, and universal character are not taken into account. As a result, this presentation is divided into two parts. The first will deal with the general question of the *Christian view of war*. The second part will deal with the more specific question of the *individual's response* to the question of war.

The treatment of the subject matter, of course, could be very different. What is said here is not exhaustive, nor is this the last word to be written on the subject from an Orthodox perspective. Moreover, much in this article has been said by others and the indebtedness of the author of these lines makes very little of what is written unique, fresh, or radically new. It is hoped, however, that what is presented here will provide

the reader with some insights and views that may contribute
to some more objective perspectives on the current situation.

The Christian View of War

In this section, three themes will be discussed: (a) the
ethics of war; (b) war as an international phenomenon; and
(c) the three classic Christian answers to the question of
Christian involvement in war. These are obviously difficult
topics, and we can only deal here with selected aspects of the
issues.

An Ethical Analysis of War. Many people are able to look
upon war and extol its benefits and its contributions to culture, science, and progress.[4] Most Christians would disagree
with this approach. I propose to defend the proposition that
by "internal definition" war is immoral. By "internal definition" I mean to say that when we look at the phenomenon
of war, we do not simply impose some external standards
and criteria upon that phenomenon. In that sense I also believe we could say that war is immoral, e.g., from the point
of view of its consequences (the destruction of human lives,
the destruction of art, culture, civilization, the disruption of
society, the cultivation of hatred, etc.). But, of course, by the
same token, others have seen benefits arising out of war
(freedom, national self-determination, heroism, defense of
the lives of the innocent, scientific advances, etc.), which
could lead to a more positive assessment of war from an
ethical point of view. When the question of the morality of
war *per se* is pursued from this point of view it can be
ambiguous.

Beyond such considerations, however, it is possible to view
the very existence, action, and prosecution of war as immoral
by "internal definition." What is meant by this term? War
is one way by which nations, and the people who make up

---

[4]There is a good treatment of the classic argument of the Prussian general
Karl von Clausewitz (1780-1831) in favor of this view in Michael Walzer,
Just and Unjust Wars: A Moral Argument with Historical Illustrations
(New York: Basic Books, 1977) 23-5.

nations, deal with and relate to each other in a particular circumstance. If moral categories are used to answer the question of *how* people relate to each other in the prosecution of any war, the one thing that we discover is that between combatants there is no recognition of normal moral claims. The old adage says that "all is fair in love and war." It is not clear that this adage is a true statement in any case, but one thing that we seem to be fairly clear about is that in the case of war, normal moral criteria and standards, which direct and guide our actions toward other people under *usual* circumstances, are arrested and put aside. In war we explicitly enter into a relationship with other people in which we recognize few if any moral claims by our opponents upon our behavior. This is an analytical, ethical definition of war. The only thing that counts in war, as war, is *victory*. In consequence, those kinds of actions condemned as immoral in normal peacetime relationships with persons of another nation—killing them, for example—are radically changed in war into a duty. Whereas one recognizes a peacetime moral requirement of compassion for other people, in war this same act may be considered a weakness; to be moved by compassion in dealing with the enemy so long as the enemy is capable of acting destructively is a poor military tactic. War then, ethically speaking, is the *mutual abrogation of the normal moral claims* that opponents have upon their antagonists' behavior.

In a sense all situations can be seen in the light of moral claims of persons and states upon each other. If we agree that human beings, as human beings, *ought* to deal morally with each other, then it becomes clear that when, in war, we refuse to respond to our opponents' claims upon us we act immorally. Thus, when we say that war is morally evil we are not simply saying that by some external criterion war is judged to be immoral; rather, we are saying that this is the very definition of war.

But the subject cannot be left there. It is altogether fair and accurate to present the Christian ethic as assessing war to be a moral evil,[5] but war is a complex phenomenon and

[5] See Cecil John Cadoux, *The Early Church and the World* (Edinburgh: T. & T. Clarke, 1955) 55, and cf. K. D. Georgoulis' article on war,

even its moral dimensions transcend what has been said above. In fact, war is a very clear example of the various "levels of moral relationships" that can be discerned in all situations. War, which is in essence an immoral confrontation of two military powers neither of which recognizes the moral claims of the other, contains within itself a whole range of human relationships that may be seen in moral terms. A level of behavior just one step removed from the refusal to recognize any moral claim upon us is the level of *retribution*, that of the "lex talionis." Its motto is "an eye for an eye and a tooth for a tooth." An army is a body of soldiers organized into units, each with a leader who is responsible for the activities and the interests of the group of combatants under him. Military discipline requires absolute obedience to the leader. If any of the soldiers would dare to contravene the orders of his immediate superior, it would be understood as a threat to the unit's safety and efficiency. Under such conditions military law is clear: the offender is subject to immediate and summary execution, since his disobedience threatens the viability of the unit. Since he does not obey orders, the officer in charge, if not able to restrain the offender, must kill him.

Beyond this level of retribution, the military situation can move to another level: that of *mutual responsibility*. This is seen among the members of a military unit in which each individual acts for the mutual well-being of the whole on the basis of self-interest. Each soldier must carry his share of the load; he must be trustworthy, so that the others can depend upon him to do what he says he will do. Here, obviously, we are on another level of moral responsibility. Men are trusting each other and putting their lives in the hands of other men. Each man senses his share of personal responsibility for the safety and well-being of his fellow soldiers.

Finally, there may come the time when the soldier moves to the highest level of moral activity, i.e., when he chooses *to sacrifice his own life* so that others might live. It was Jesus who said, "Greater love hath no man than to give his life for his brother." The classic story of the soldier who

"Πόλεμος," in the Θρησκευτικὴ καὶ Ἠθικὴ Ἐγκυκλοπαίδεια 10 (Athens, 1967) 494.

throws himself on a hand grenade in order to protect the lives of his comrades is an example of self-sacrificing love of the highest moral quality. No duty requires this, no officer can command it, yet a man may do this freely out of self-sacrificing love.

The war situation, then, includes within itself the possibility for all kinds of levels of moral actions, but war itself, *as war*, is by definition an immoral situation. If this premise is accepted, we can then proceed and ask the question, What is the place of war in the arena of international politics?

War as an International Phenomenon. There are some cases (which I will mention below) that do not fit the pattern I am now going to describe, but I think that the vast majority of wars do fit this pattern. In most cases, wars are a sign that nations have failed through other means—diplomatic, economic, and social—to resolve their differences. Nations, in our age, think of themselves as autonomous political entities whose purpose it is to act in international relations for their own benefit, and seek to enhance their well-being and interests through acts of diplomacy. Thus, civil leaders, the magistrates of the nation-state, enter into diplomatic ties essentially for the prosecution of the narrowly conceived well-being of their respective nations. All international governmental functions are undertaken in this light: diplomacy, economic pacts, political treaties, population exchanges. But, finally, if two nations feel that their claims to justice, or their claims for the well-being of their citizenry or their "national interests," however defined, are at odds with each other, and that every other means has been more or less exhausted, then war is perceived to be their last resort for resolving the dispute. This is how war has historically functioned. Regardless of whatever else government is, one of the absolute necessities for a government to function is that it be able to exercise power, i.e., military force. Therefore, government, which exercises this power through the militia, the police, and the military forces to maintain order among its own citizenry, at times also exercises that power upon *other* nations. War is seen as a *power* issue and *not* an issue of morality. It is not, in practical politics, a question of *right and wrong!*[6]

This understanding of war comes back to our earlier definition by another route. When governments finally become convinced that they are not going to gain what they want through the accepted moral channels of diplomacy, and finally move to a point where they feel that the continuation of this kind of effort will not achieve acceptable results, they enter into war. War, then, is a rejection of those other means. Thus, war takes itself out of the picture of legal, moral control. The weakest legal system in existence is that of international law, and the weakest part of international law is that element of it which deals with how nations *come* to war. As poor as they are, the provisions that deal with how wars are to be conducted are much more widely recognized and accepted than the regulations that seek to define how nations should "legally" enter into war. We have the "Geneva Convention," for example, dealing with the treatment of prisoners of war, which most nations are willing to abide by, but we have very few laws on the international level that control or guide the nations as to how they shall *enter* into war.

Now, in this fundamentally immoral, yet very real situation, which is part and parcel of the way nations have been dealing with each other over the whole of recorded human history, the Christian comes to make judgment. And Christians have found it possible to look at this phenomenon in at least three ways. To these, and a criticism of them, we now turn.

Three Classic Christian Responses. A man who has made perhaps one of the most important studies of Christian attitudes toward war, Roland Bainton, has presented us with a typology which, if simplified, points to the three distinct answers Christians have given to the reality called war.[7] The

---

[6] A discussion of this argument as it applied to the dropping of the first atomic bomb can be found in Richard A. Wasserstrom, ed., *War and Morality* (Belmont, Calif.: Wadsworth, 1970) 78-101.

[7] Roland H. Bainton, *Christian Attitudes toward War and Peace: A Historical Survey and Critical Reevaluation* (New York: Abingdon, 1960).

three answers are *pacifism*, the *just war theory*, and the *crusade*. *Pacifism* is the position that holds when the Christian has taken a stance of refusal to participate in war. In this view, the agent of war, the state, is usually thought of as evil, and therefore the Christian ought to have little or nothing to do with the state in general. As a consequence, the Christian finds it possible to separate himself from the state and commit his whole life to a pacifistic position regarding war. He refuses to serve in war; he refuses to contribute to the propagation and the development of wars. For the pacifist, both war and the state that propagates war are immoral. This answer requires radical separation from both.[8]

The second position is the *just war theory*. It is probably the most misunderstood and maligned view, but one that all persons are driven to consider when they begin thinking about the issue of war. The first thing that needs to be pointed out is that this is not a theory that whitewashes war. It is not the theory of the *good* war; it is the *just* war theory. In no case when Christians talk about a just war theory do they consider that they transform the inherently evil aspect of war into some objective moral good. War continues to be an evil, simply because it is an embodiment of everything that God does not want men to do. Thus, when we consider a just war theory, we speak about a theory that seeks to deal with something already recognized as immoral, and in dealing with it, perhaps to mitigate its evils. The just war theory holds that war is an evil and seeks to make it *less* evil. And so, depending upon its particular form, there are at least two types of thinking, in two areas to which we have already referred. The first set of ideas refers to questions *ad bellum*, i.e., the issues related to how nations are to *enter into war*. Authors such as St. Augustine, or more recent writers on the subject such as Paul Ramsey, Professor of Christian Ethics at Princeton, who has done a great deal to rehabilitate the

For a useful survey of current attitudes to the issue of war and ethics see also the "Bibliographical Essay" in Ralph B. Potter, *War and Moral Discourse* (Richmond, Va.: John Knox Press, 1969) 87-123.

[8]For a classification of various pacifistic positions, see Guy Franklin Hershberger, *War, Peace, and Nonresistance* (Scottdale, Pa.: Herald Press, 1944).

just war theory, have dealt with the issue of *ad bellum* moral criteria.[9] These criteria seek to delineate the conditions under which a nation is justified in entering into war with another nation. And considerations such as defense from attack and the protection of the innocent lead most just war theorists to cast their discussions in terms of a defensive war.

In addition to the question of *jus ad bellum*, we also have questions dealing with what is morally *permissible* and *prohibited* when involved in a war, i.e., the question of *jus in bellum*. The criteria developed to answer this question deal with the limits of force, the issue of noncombatant populations, the extent of defeat imposed upon a conquered enemy, legitimate and nonlegitimate targets, etc. Most people do not realize that both the Nuremberg trials after the Second World War and the trials of the American officers regarding the My Lai massacres after the Vietnam War are concrete instances of just war theories in the process of application. Specifically, the My Lai trials were *not* on the issue of whether the Vietnam War was a just or unjust war. Rather, the issue was whether in the propagation of that war something like My Lai was right or wrong. It was an issue of what is permitted *in bellum*.[10] Thus, many Christians have involved themselves in that kind of problem, accepting the fact that we live in a world under the sway of the devil, that in "this age" we live and are constantly under the influence of the "Prince of this age," and that one of the facts of that reign of evil is "wars and rumors of wars." They ask: Since we live in this kind of world, what do we do as Christians to limit, and restrict, that which is admitted to be evil and immoral? The answer is cast in the form of a "just war theory."

The third answer that Christians have developed is the *crusade*, in which war is seen as a positive good. It must be admitted that although nearly all Christian bodies have experienced a "crusade mentality" at certain points during their

[9]Paul Ramsey, *The Just War: Force and Political Responsibility* (New York: Charles Scribner's Sons, 1968). See also his *War and the Christian Conscience: How Shall Modern War Be Conducted Justly?* (Durham, N. C.: Duke University Press, 1961).

[10]Walzer, cited above, provides his readers with a thorough treatment of *jus in bellum*.

histories, the East in general has been comparatively free of it. Perhaps, as Ostrogorsky says, the "forerunner of the later crusades" in Christian history was the Emperor Heraclius' campaign against the Persians (622-630),[11] but it is also true that there was nothing again approaching a crusade in the subsequent history of the Byzantine empire. Ostrogorsky notes that "the crusading movement as the West conceived it was something entirely foreign to the Byzantine empire. There was nothing new in a war against the infidel, but to the Byzantines, this was the outcome of hard political necessity."[12] The Byzantines preferred to keep the peace through negotiations, the payment of tribute, intrigue, and common military activity. They were not crusaders. It was the West that developed the crusade into a religious and international policy.

In this case, war is almost completely purged of its evil aspects and presented as a good and noble means for the achievement of some good and noble purpose. Usually the purpose is presented as a religious one, though we can speak of secularized "crusades," which might well be a good description of World War II.

> A crusade is a war fought for religious or ideological purposes. It aims not at defense or law enforcement, but at the creation of new political orders and at mass conversions. It is the international equivalent of religious persecution and political repression, and it is obviously ruled out by the argument for justice. Yet the very existence of Nazism tempts us as it tempted General Eisenhower, to imagine World War II as a "crusade in Europe." So we must draw the line between just wars and crusades as cleary as we can.[13]

Men are made to feel that they are acting righteously, doing good things, when they enter into this kind of war. The

[11]George Ostrogorsky, *History of the Byzantine State* (New Brunswick, N. J.: Rutgers University Press, 1957) 90.

[12]Ibid., p. 320. See also Demetrios Constantelos, *Byzantine Philanthropy and Social Welfare* (New Brunswick, N. J.: Rutgers Byzantine Series, 1968) 41, 50, 123, 126, 135.

[13]Walzer, pp. 113-4.

consequence is that the crusade is praised, accepted as a positive good, and people are taught that they are acting righteously when they participate in it.

Before proceeding, we have to ask the question: How adequate are these Christian responses to the question of war? I think that each of them may embody a *portion* of Christian value and Christian truth, yet each of them actually also serves to *subvert* aspects of Christian truth. Let us look first at pacifism. Without question, pacifism seeks to emphasize the separateness of the Christian from the evil in the world and seeks to call Christians to an absolute commitment to the words of Christ. One cannot help but observe that this approach is heroic, even though perhaps unrealistic and impractical inasmuch as there is no known case in the history of the world in which nations committed to going to war with each other have been altered from their courses of action by pacifists. The logical and practical result of the pacifist position is that the pacifist's nation is defeated. As a consequence, it flies in the face of the Christian call for order in society and protection of the weak and the innocent, which is as much a demand of Christian teaching as is the idea of nonviolence.

But the just war theory is also vulnerable to criticism. The just war theory seeks to achieve some kind of comprehensive picture, and as a consequence we can say that in international law there has been an attempt to provide some humanizing and ethical dimensions to the phenomenon of war by just war considerations. But here we have to admit the fact that in spite of some restraining effects the just war theory has not been overly successful in eliminating or reducing wars. At the same time, it provides a tremendous compromise with other Christian values. While permitting the Christian to support the maintenance of civil order, to defend the innocent and the weak, and to uphold justice, it concurrently turns away from those principles for which Jesus was best known: that we love one another, that we maintain the fundamental morality of the Decalogue, that we cultivate patience, kindness, gentleness, that we turn the other cheek. It seems to slight that dimension of the Christian teaching while emphasizing the other.

The third Christian alternative, that of the crusade, also shows some of the same kind of ambiguity. It teaches that arms *should* be taken up for the sake of some very just cause; that evil *should* be put down not only with words but in reality; that only force can accomplish this since evil reigns by force; that the heroic battle of good and evil may require the use of military force. Certainly, destroying and conquering evil is a very powerful Christian motif. However, the crusade serves to sacrifice a tremendous number of other values in the process. One of the values thus put down is the obvious requirement that Christians ought to be the makers of peace rather than the makers of war. The Byzantines, like the ancient Jews, always thought of their battles as divinely led, and both were very confident that as they went out into battle God was with them, even though they might not have literally thought of their wars as "crusades." It was in the western medieval period that this kind of war was raised up to a supernational phenomenon, an ideal combining religious and military (not to mention economic and commercial) factors. But the shortcomings of the crusade from the Christian point of view are so obvious and evident that there is no need to dwell upon them here.

Thus, what we have is a set of three possible answers that do not respond to the question of Christian responsibility in war in an entirely satisfactory manner, since they do not individually serve to realize all of the Christian values. This seems to point to the fact that there are structured within our Christian faith a substantial number of tensions, each pulling upon the others as we face this issue (and, it would seem, practically any other issue). The call for Christians is, then, first and above all, *not to oversimplify*; not to make the question too easy to solve. Experience shows that when there are easy answers to complex questions, there are always difficult consequences. In the case of war this is especially true. We ought not simplify an extremely complex problem, with which Christians have been struggling and attempting to answer for all of the two millenia of our history.

But of the answers we have given up until this time, none have managed to conserve, protect, promote, and elevate all Christian values. There is a fundamental reason for this, arising from those self-same values and teachings. The Christian reason for this is, of course, that we find ourselves "between the times"; we live in this "present age," and the Kingdom, in which God will rule in peace, love, and justice and the lamb and the lion will rest together, is yet to come. This is the real cause of this ambiguous and compromising situation. The affirmation of the imperfection and compromised aspect of anything we do in this world does not permit in the practical real-life situation of international relations a completely satisfactory answer.[14] With that as background, then, we may now move to the question of the individual Christian's response to the question of war.

The Individual Christian's Response

The second part of this paper addresses itself to the individual's personal response to the question of war. Here, too, we will touch on three topics: (a) the New Testament commandment of nonviolence; (b) the Church's "stratification" of pacifism; and (c) an outline of how individual Christians can personally respond to the question of war.

The New Testament Commandment of Nonviolence. The most honest and correct place to start a discussion such as this is with the New Testament source of the issue. Unlike Islam, for instance, or even the Old Testament, the New Testament never praises nor enjoins violent military activity. The issue, however, is brought to a very sharp focus for Christians in a special way that transcends questions of good will or humanitarian considerations: by the explicit and rigorous commands of Jesus to His followers as recorded in the Sermon on the Mount. It is the New Testament itself, which—if we may state it in this way—creates the problem for the Christian involved in the day-to-day process of living and decision making in the world. When the Christian is

[14]See Walzer's comments in ibid., p. 329, which are particularly illuminating, coming from a secular perspective.

asked to define what, *as a Christian*, his attitude to war is, he is necessarily forced back to chapter 5 of the Gospel of Matthew. Jesus' teaching is not limited to the Old Testament commandment, "Thou shalt do no murder." Both for civil law and the Christian conscience murder is something definable. All taking of life is *not* murder. To be specific, we are able to determine several degrees of murder, as exemplified in the legal designation of first, second, and third degree murder. For example, the *defense* of one's life from an unprovoked and unjustified attack is not only permitted to the Christian, it is his *duty*; and if that defense requires the killing of the attacker, it is no murder. But most Christians, if they take the question of war and peace seriously, will finally settle on Christ's teaching of nonresistance as the critical value.

The Christian must come to some understanding of what this commandment and this teaching mean for the question of war. Though familiar, the relevant passages can be repeated here, in order to emphasize their centrality for the issue.

> You have heard that it was said, "An eye for an eye and a tooth for a tooth." But I say to you, Do not resist one who is evil. But if any one strikes you on the right cheek, turn to him the other also; and if any one would sue you and take your coat, let him have your cloak as well; and if any one forces you to go one mile, go with him two miles. Give to him who begs from you and do not refuse him who would borrow from you.

> You have heard that it was said, "You shall love your neighbor and hate your enemy." But I say to you, Love your enemies and pray for those who persecute you, so that you may be sons of your Father who is in heaven; for he makes his sun rise on the evil and on the good, and sends rain on the just and on the unjust. For if you love those who love you, what reward have you? (Matt. 5:38-46)

Love your enemies, do good to those who hate you,
bless those who curse you, pray for those who abuse
you. To him who strikes you on the cheek, offer the
other also; and from him who takes away your cloak
do not withhold your coat as well. Give to every one
who begs from you; and of him who takes away your
goods, do not ask them again. And as you wish that
men would do to you, do so to them.

If you love those who love you what credit is that to
you?... But love your enemies, and do good, and
lend, expecting nothing in return; and your reward
will be great, and you will be sons of the Most High;
for he is kind to the ungrateful and the selfish. Be
merciful, even as your Father is merciful. (Luke
6:27-32, 35-36)

For many Christians, these passages create a sentimental
mood, a warmth of goodness, which impresses us as "beautiful" and "sweet." But this teaching of nonresistance, nonviolence, and returning good for evil has also always been a
stumbling block for those Christians seeking to live a real
Christian life in the real world, in which so much force,
violence, evil, and destructiveness exist. The "down to earth"
practical man hears it and scoffs: "This is a utopian teaching; how foolish: how could this kind of teaching function
in a real world? Jesus is a visionary when he asks people to
function this way. If someone attacks me and hits me on the
head, I'm supposed to turn around and let him hit me on the
back too? You're crazy!" he will conclude.

Jesus was, however, much more profound than those of
us who look upon these words in a mood of sentimentality
and say "how beautiful—if only it could be," and He was
much more practical than those who would call His teaching
"foolish impracticality." Jesus knew well of what He spoke,
and He knew exactly what He was saying. He was neither
talking in riddles nor was He talking in terms of some kind
of unrealizable ideal. The principle of nonviolence that Jesus
taught in His Sermon on the Mount is an important principle

for human relationships. And it is a fundamental working principle that can be applied in all spheres of human relationships. It is practical and realizable. Jesus knew and communicated one very simple fact: that in human relations, *like attitudes create like attitudes*. He knew, for example, that if a person enters a room full of strangers and behaves in an angry, grouchy, critical manner, he will soon create in all of those present the same kind of attitudes toward him. Every person has had situations at home, in groups, and at work that testify to this universal human phenomenon. When an associate is angry and grouchy, that attitude seems to be readily communicated to others, and even if one tries to stop that person from acting angrily, it is quite likely that one will become angry himself in the process! It seems to be a rule of life that negative, antagonistic, hate-filled or even antagonistic-appearing behavior seems to create the same kind of attitude in others. This pattern tends to reinforce itself as it goes along. Through escalating repetition it creates a vicious circle of hatred and misunderstanding.

We can create an imaginary situation to illustrate what is meant here. Two strangers are walking down the hall. A quite accidentally and unconsciously bumps against the shoulder of B. B notices it and looks at A in a quizzical manner. "I wonder why he bumped into me," he says. B may have some problems of his own and may see this event as an expression of antagonism. Later, B and A meet in different circumstances, and A greets B in a normal way but B responds a little coldly, slightly suspicious and sensitive to A's greeting. A senses the tension and distance between himself and B and feels resentful. Before long A decides that he doesn't like B, though, admittedly, he doesn't know why. Future events bring them together again. At each meeting the antagonism escalates. A will find in B's coldness and abrupt remarks justification for increasingly hostile attitudes on his part toward A. Naturally, B responds in like manner. The situation escalates more and more in a pattern of "dislike creating dislike," which intensifies as the experience increases. A vicious circle of hatred has been created.

Now, the question arises: How does one go about changing that kind of situation? How does one stop the escalating, negative vicious circle? In order for the situation to change, there has to be an abrupt about-face. *Someone* has to stop returning evil for evil. *Someone* has to decide to change this relationship into a "good for evil" relationship. *Someone* has to decide not to respond in kind, but to respond kindly. And what would be the consequence? Like begets like. Attitudes begin to change. Negative attitudes are slowly neutralized. A series of "good" responses to "not so good" actions may begin changing the character of the relationship between A and B. The tension of their relationship begins to "wind down." Where enmity was now comes a minimal amount of tolerance; where tolerance was might come kindness; and where kindness exists, there might come love.

Jesus was no visionary when he spoke of "turning the other cheek." He was practical and realistic. Jesus' principle of returning good for evil is a principle that works, is real and practicable.

This understanding of the biblical injunction to return good for evil finds application to the question of war. As we have seen, there is no moral relationship in war. War is precisely the condition between nations in which evil is consistently returned for evil. Ever-increasing retribution, until one of the combatants is forced to submit, is its prime characteristic. Thus, war is the denial of the proposition of Christlike nonviolent action and the returning of good for evil. Christ's principle of returning good for evil does not fit—by definition—in what we call a situation of war. But, if that is the case, we are then really faced with a dilemma. If war *means* that one nation accepts no moral responsibility for the enemy nation, and that it recognizes no moral claims by the enemy upon its own behavior, then returning good for evil is *not* a possibility to combatant nations, since that kind of action is a response to mutually recognized moral claims. *It is not possible to return good for evil and still be at war!* Thus, if a nation is at war with another nation, it cannot be responding to these moral claims.[15]

[15]The presupposition of a moral climate and moral relationships is also seen in the exercise of civil disobedience. Civil disobedience in Mahatma

That is the tragedy, and that is what gives Christians the problem of how the individual faces such a dilemma. However, in history Christians and the Church have had to respond somehow to this dilemma and to this response I now would like to turn for a brief analysis.

The Church's Stratification of Pacifism. The Church's response to this dilemma has been to "stratify" the pacifist response. In short, the Church decided to require monks and clergy to be the pacifists in a Church which spoke for the whole of society! Thus, canon 83 of the Apostolic Canons says that a priest or bishop may not engage in military matters. Also prohibited to clergy is government service,[16] because one thereby compromises his priesthood. Canon 7 of the Fourth Ecumenical Council combines both injunctions: "We have decreed in regard to those who have once been enrolled in the Clergy or who have become Monks shall not join the army nor obtain any secular position of dignity. Let those be anathematized who dare to do this and fail to repent, so as to return to that which they had previously chosen on God's account." The commentary in the *Rudder* interprets this as very broad based: ". . . clergymen and monks must not become soldiers, nor assume secular dignities."[17] But why is it that Apostolic Canon 83 only deposes these men from office, whereas this canon anathematizes them? The former canon

Ghandi's India proved to be successful because the English rulers maintained a sense of moral relatedness with the Indians whom they ruled. Martin Luther King's efforts also appealed to a moral conscience. Thus, John Rawls, in his *A Theory of Justice* (Oxford: Clarendon Press, 1972) writes that civil disobedience "addresses the sense of justice of the community." However, such efforts in the Soviet Union fail because, ideologically, those seeking civil and religious liberties are perceived to be outside the moral framework of the state as described by Marxist ideology. There is no moral community between the Marxist state and the dissenters. Consequently, their repression and elimination of the dissenters is not only easily accepted and justified ("enemies of the people"), but carried out with the moral certitude of a crusade. The parallel with the war situation as defined in this article is clearly evident.

[16]Canon 6 and canon 81. See also canon 3 of the Fourth Ecumenical Council and canon 10 of the Seventh Ecumenical Council.

[17]Agapius and Nikodemos, *The Rudder*, tr. D. Cummings (Chicago: Orthodox Christian Education Society, 1957) 252.

is referring to those who engage in such things *while* wearing the habit of the clergy, whereas the present canon is speaking of those who discard even the clergyman's or monk's habit before engaging in such things.[18] This attitude is illustrated by many episodes in the history of the Church, one of which was reported by the twelfth-century canonist Balsamon while commenting on some writings of St. Basil. It seems that some priests and laypersons had become involved in battle and had killed people. Some of these priests were then brought before a synod of bishops. Certain of the bishops charged the priests with murder and asked that they be defrocked and prohibited from functioning as priests, as their actions sullied the purity of their priesthood. However, the majority of the bishops at the synod responded differently. Given the circumstances of the case, though they deplored the fact that the killings had taken place, they judged the priests' acts as—if not right—at least unavoidable and therefore voted that they were not to be defrocked. But laymen were not tried! The implications of this story are of interest for our inquiry. Priests, because they are close to the altar, and monks, because they have separated themselves from the world, are kept isolated from the normal rules and functioning of society.

Such a distinction between what is expected of priests and monks and what is expected of the "average" Christian is not limited to the question of participation in war. Yet, the issue would be much more tenable were we willing in the rest of our theology to draw a very sharp line between the laity and the priests. If theology was ready to teach that there is a set of ethics for the priest and a completely different one for the layman, then such a stratification of pacifism might be justified. If theology was prepared to say that the "pure Church" is the priests and the other Christians are "less than full members of the Church," one could justify the distinction between pacifist priests and monks and nonpacifist lay people. And for a long time both priests and lay people have accepted this kind of "stratification" within the Church.

But recently, the Orthodox have begun to recognize and

[18]Ibid.

to emphasize the role of the laity in the Church. The Church has recognized the fact that the Church is not just the priests and monks, but is the "people of God," including the laity. The Church is the total body of the believers, and all of us, gathered together on Sunday morning at the Divine Liturgy, are the manifestation of the Kingdom of God. We are all the Church.[19] Consequently, if the Church is required to emphasize the unity of the body of the Church as including both the laity and the clergy, then it would seem to follow that the pacifistic alternative available for the clergyman might *also* be available for the layperson. If we are to hold that the clergy should not, by virtue of their office, bear arms, the Church must in some way or another permit, allow, and justify for the laity the option of the *same* alternative.

A consequence of this is that a new burden is placed on the shoulders of the layperson. Each Christian is going to have to opt for one of the three alternatives with which Christians have traditionally responded to the question of war. *Pacifism, just war,* or *crusade* answers now become free *alternatives* for the Orthodox Christian. The likelihood of choosing the crusade as an answer these days is slim, and I think that the Orthodox Christian mentality would find this alternative the least congenial. Orthodox Christians, however, do have a real choice in this day and age between the remaining two: the pacifistic answer, and the just war answer.

The Individual Response. It appears likely that the vast majority of Orthodox Christians would opt for a kind of "just war theory" regarding the involvement of Christians in war. Most Christians will keep in mind the fact of the imperfections of our political systems, the need to defend one's life, to protect the weak, to defend the innocent against the ravages of immoral behavior of military conquerers upon the defeated, and perhaps above all, the desire and right to freedom and self-determination. Certainly, this has been the gen-

---

[19]This is a universal emphasis of modern Orthodox theology. See, for example, Nicholas Afanassief, "The Ministry of the Laity of the Church," *Ecumenical Review* 10 (1958) 30-8; and my book *Living the Liturgy* (Minneapolis: Light and Life, 1974) 47-50.

eral position held by most Greek Orthodox ethicists.[20] Keeping these values foremost, most Christians would see war as an unavoidable evil and opt for some form of "just war" theory focusing on the idea of defensive, as opposed to offensive war. These Christians will expend their efforts to work out international machinery to mediate disputes between nations, to uproot the social causes of war, to seek to clarify and limit the *jus ad bellum* and the *jus in bellum*, and in general to make what is in actuality happening among nations less frequent in occurrence and more humane in exercise. Most Orthodox Christians, as Christians, are going to be realistic enough with regard to national authority to go along with being drafted, or joining the military service, and serving their country in the military. All of this takes place in the context of a "just war" response, in which "war" is seen as a lesser evil and not as a positive good. Some Orthodox Christians are going to be so impressed by the claims of "order" and "justice" and "the realities" that they are going to make careers out of serving in the military forces. For them, the armed forces are a "stop-gate" to all kinds of evil disorder and injustice.

Every Christian, however, who takes this option must realize that a free pass to every kind of behavior does *not* go with it. Anyone who has been to war, or who has learned what happens during war, knows that "war is hell." In my research at the Harvard library on the subject of this paper I found in the card catalogue a book entitled *Morals and War*. Since the title looked promising, I inquired where the book was, and I was directed to the "old part" of the library. In the stacks on the top floor, among some dusty books which appeared not to have been touched for decades, I found the book and hurriedly checked it out to peruse later at home, noticing that the last time the book was taken out was over four years before. As I began to read, I discovered that the word "Morals" in the title did not refer to the ethical issues of war, but to "sex"! *Morals and War* is a book about the sexual behavior of military people during war! It was not pleasant reading. The book describes violations of innocent women, horrible, dehumanizing brothels, women and children brutalized in battle situations, and so much more. This relatively insignificant aspect of war, precisely because it is so generally discounted, lifted up some of the terror and the fearfulness of the concurrent aspects of war. It is not only the killing that is evil. What war also does to a whole population, to human decency and dignity, to life and the quality of life makes one shudder. Christians who go to war in terms of a just war alternative are then obligated to make sure that whatever they do in war they must do as *Christians*, paradoxical as that may appear. There are many things that persons can do in war that cannot be justified by a just war doctrine. This is the implication of serious concern with the *jus in bellum* aspects of the just war approach. The decision to accept the just war approach requires moral sensitivity and careful ethical judgment.

But there are some Christians who will not be able to accept the just war approach to this question. Some Christians will be committed to a total nonviolent approach to war simply because they are Christians and want to emphasize the perfection demanded by the Christian calling. Those who do this recognize that they open themselves up to the charge and the danger that the innocent and weak may suffer from their action, that evil may take place because they choose not to lift the sword in defense. There are people who will do this in the total context of life. They will seek to live their lives completely in a nonviolent fashion.

As in the case of the monasteries in Byzantium, the United States as a nation has recognized in its laws the right of conscientious objection. The traditional "peace churches" have always had this privilege. If a person, from the beginning of his adult life, declared that he was a conscientious objector, he could readily become exempt from military service. If he showed this by being a member of a church that was totally committed to this type of thinking, then our government traditionally has granted him immunity from the requirement of bearing arms. In 1967 the draft law was interpreted by the Supreme Court to exempt anyone from military service "whose consciences, spurred by deeply held moral, ethical, or religious beliefs, would give them no rest or peace if they allowed themselves to become a part of an instrument of war."[21]

If an Orthodox Christian, not belonging to a historic "peace church," decides that he cannot participate in war because of the Christian principle of nonviolence, then *everything* in his life must show his commitment to this principle. Traditionally, this has meant the monastery. It need not mean that today, it would appear. But certainly the style of life that a person chooses should be in harmony with the nonviolent affirmation. If he is going to make this commitment as a Christian, his life must be the kind of life that will bear up under the scrutiny of a nonviolent criterion. In such a case an Orthodox Christian could not appear before a draft board and say, "I'm an Orthodox Christian, and though my Church isn't pacifistic, I am a pacifist, but I love going to wrestling matches, enjoy rifle practice and hunting, and constantly enjoy the boxing matches on television." Obviously this is a ludicrous example, but it serves to illustrate what is meant when a pacifist (in reference to military service) is ethically required to commit his total life to the principle of nonviolence. Such a consistent stance would be generally acceptable both in our American society and in the Orthodox Church at large, it would appear.[22] There are, however, other nations that do not recognize this right. This has to be noted because the issue becomes so much sharper in the next instance, the case of "selective conscientious objection."

Some people have been claiming *for themselves* since the Vietnam War the right to decide whether a particular war is just or unjust and to choose whether they can morally par-

[21]As reported in *Time* (March 22, 1971) 52.

[22]Both Androutsos and Antoniades reject the principle of conscientious objection. Antoniades particularly rejects the idea of selective conscientious objection. The latter's view is based primarily on the lack of appropriate knowledge and responsibility on the part of the individual citizen. His appeal to "obedience to conscience" here appears particularly weak and unacceptable in that he understands it only as requiring obedience to authority. Antoniades, pp. 138-9.

ticipate or not in a particular war. That claim was challenged in the courts of our nation. It is obvious why it was challenged: the civic leaders who make the *jus ad bellum* decisions would be in a very grave and weakened position in terms of the defense of the nation if they left the choice of fighting to the citizens themselves. Few were surprised that the courts did not ultimately permit selective conscientious objection and that it was decisively rejected by the Supreme Court in 1971. However, it is still an option for an Orthodox Christian, if he is willing to pay the price. Should the draft be reestablished, selective conscientious objection is still a moral and spiritual option, but it must be as the acceptance of a cross; it cannot be taken without the readiness to accept its consequences. Just as Christ died on the cross as a consequence of his own sense of mission for the world's salvation, in the same way, Christians who ultimately are going to follow the way of selective conscientious objection will have to pay. That is the way it is. What is unacceptable is a "weasel morality," which would refuse service in the armed forces for ethical reasons and yet not be willing to pay the consequences; to receive the benefits of a nation's strength and well-being, political and international position, without giving service in return. Though it was unpopular, the post-Vietnam amnesty plan, requiring some minimal expression of service for refusal to serve in the armed forces, was based on sound ethical principles. The indignation of the selective conscientious objectors to the plan was in fact based on the view that some wars could be good and right, though the Vietnam War was not. It is this which makes their view in the last analysis unacceptable.[23]

Conclusion

Given this controversy, is there something that all of us, pacifists and nonpacifists, need to do at this time? Yes, we

[23]See my article "Christian Thinking on Amnesty," in Stanley S. Harakas (Exetastes), *Contemporary Issues* (New York: Greek Orthodox Archdiocese Press, 1976) 88-90.

all have a commonly shared moral obligation to do whatever we can to avoid war and to encourage peace. The first thing we can do as Christians is to *pray*. Orthodox Christians need only refer to their service books for this. The Divine Liturgy of St. John Chrysostom contains a reference to the word "peace" on practically every page. When one considers the amazing number of words in the language, or even if one were to consider only the religious words, this is an extremely high incidence of concern for peace. The Divine Liturgy as a model for prayer places a high priority upon peace.

More, of course, needs to be done in the light of the Orthodox doctrine of *synergy*. Christians should take the initiative to promote in the world in which they live the peace-bringing spirit that belongs to Christ. The first thing that we have to recognize as we do this is that we live in a pluralistic age. We are one group among other groups, but we can join our forces in efforts such as this with others—Christians and non-Christians who are interested in furthering the cause of peace. We are *not* the "powers that be" in most cases. We can only influence the powers that be. However, it is our Orthodox Christian ethical duty to act in this way, especially in the democracies of the West where religious values are accepted by those in positions of authority.

Secondly, we can look to the real *causes* of war, which are to be found in the economic and social injustices that exist throughout the world. For instance, Americans must ask themselves how it is that we can have such a small percentage of the world's population and use up to forty percent of its energy? How can we justify our own use of sixty percent of the oil supply of the world? We are now beginning to question whether we must continuously have the bigger and more powerful automobiles. Can we not think in terms of spending our resources for the benefit and welfare of the poverty-stricken and hungry peoples of other nations? Again the president has asked for an increase in foreign aid, nearly all of which is for military hardware. That is tragic compared to the humanitarian and constructive foreign aid of this richest of all nations, which is less than one percent of our gross national product. Can priorities such as these make us a peace-promoting nation? Alexander Tsirindanes, a Greek Orthodox thinker whose work was favorably reviewed by Fr. Georges Florovsky,[24] however, felt that peace efforts not based on the development of international law, and internal criticism not based on criteria of justice, were not only illusory, but *harmful* as well. He writes:

> Desires for international peace which do not comprehend a state of international justice, for the sake of which we must all agree to make sacrifices, are dreams which simply prevent the defense of the wronged, and secure tolerance for the unjust. Dreams like those are nothing else but a participation in international crime.[25]

Thirdly, we Orthodox can work together in seeking to *organize* ourselves in realistic, practical, and down-to-earth projects for social renewal. Where there is less pain, less suffering, where there is less hunger, the likeliness of war is lessened. We Orthodox Christians can exercise our special vocation in the spiritualizing of things. We have a way of doing that coming out from the theology of transfiguration, which characterizes Orthodox Christianity. We can exercise, among other Christians and in the world, a mission that seeks to lead people to see the spiritual dimensions of everything that we do.

In the last analysis, there are *no* recipes to be applied in a mechanical or legalistic fashion. Never has the Christian faith, properly understood, bypassed the self-determining con-

[24]In *Christianity and Culture*, vol. 2 of the *Collected Works of Georges Florovsky* (Belmont, Mass.: Nordland, 1974) 140-2.

[25]Christian Union of Professional Men (A. Tsirindanes), *Toward a Christian Civilization* (Athens, 1950) 212. See also his book *Knowing Where We Are Going: Contemporary Problems and the Christian Faith* (London: Cassell, 1977), in which a strong appeal for Christian attention to issues of social justice is made (pp. 95-6). In addition, see the book *Christian Obedience and the Search for Liberation: An Orthodox Perspective* (Geneva: World Student Federation, 1979). These lectures and papers from the Second International Consultation of Orthodox Youth and Students in Cairo address some of the social, economic, moral, and spiritual causes of war, though not directly.

science of the person growing toward *theosis*. All that can be said is that we are in a profound and perplexing situation in which not all of the values of the Christian faith can be simultaneously realized. Ultimately we have *to make our choices among the values* that we will emphasize as regards war. This means that Christians are going to have to sacrifice one or another dimension of the Christian commitment in order to come to grips with the issue of war.

If there is one word heard more frequently in the Liturgy than "peace," it is the petition "Kyrie eleison"—"Lord have mercy." We are caught in a tragic, almost unresolvable dilemma, characteristic of all involvements of the Christian in the "world." In the case of war it is especially acute. Thus, we act and simultaneously we pray "Kyrie eleison," looking not to our own efforts, finally, for the resolution of the problem. We know that none of our problems are solved exclusively by our own efforts. We look ultimately to the grace of God and then we become very much like the early Christians, and in particular, like the writer of the New Testament book of Revelation. Together with the author of that apocalyptic work we seek a new world and we say, "I saw a new heaven and a new earth . . . and I saw the Holy City, New Jerusalem, coming down out of heaven from God . . . and I heard a great voice from the throne saying 'Behold the dwelling of God is with men. He will dwell with them and they shall be his people' " (Rev. 21:1-3). Such is our vision, our hope, our dream, and together with the first Christians as we face the problem of the individual's response to war, we can only repeat the apocalyptic cry: "Maranatha, Maranatha, Lord, come Lord." Only then will the issue be fully resolved.

CHAPTER **6**

THE SYNTHESIS OF PRAXIS AND THEORY

A cynical priest will not only destroy himself, but his community also. You were ordained in order to bring Christ to people and people to Christ.

I have told you more than once that the bishop is no longer a picture on the wall, living in some ivory tower. On the contrary, the bishop must be very much involved in the life of his sheep. Otherwise, the word "shepherd" becomes completely meaningless.

Metropolitan Philip

The synthesis of praxis and theory is the problem sui generis of pastoral theology. This chapter, therefore, is one which seeks to explicate the very nature of pastoral theology, not in some "general" form, but in how it can be seen in a distinctive, Orthodox perspective. The major thrust of this chapter is, by intent and choice, indeed an educational one. This is only proper, inasmuch as Metropolitan Philip, to whom this book is dedicated, has held pastoral theology, i.e., the question of praxis and theory, to be a crucial concern as the Church prepares to engage the twenty-first century.

It should also be noted here that this article, now presented in appropriate form for this book, has served to structure the courses in pastoral theology taught at both St. Vladimir's and Holy Cross theological schools.

J. J. A.

The "Being in Act" of Theology

by

JOSEPH J. ALLEN

In this article I would like to "share and exchange" some views concerning the problem of "pastoral theology," especially in the context of what the Orthodox pastor and seminarian need to be aware of and to learn in order to successfully fulfill their vocation. However, this does not mean that this presentation is meant solely for present or future clergymen. The Orthodox *layperson* can only benefit from an understanding of what is the pastor's role in the "pastoral" relationship and can perhaps himself pass this benefit on to fellow Christians.

The procedure I shall use in exploring this problem consists of three phases. First, we shall examine the general nature of the problem. Secondly, we shall try to discover the specific Orthodox model in the light of that problem. And from there we shall go on to look at some of the particular methods for realizing the preparation for pastoral theology.

The General Nature of the Problem

In 1977, Julian Hartt wrote something that can introduce the nature of the problem of pastoral theology. In his *Theological Method and Imagination*, he describes three motives: (1) defense of the faith; (2) exposition of the doctrines; and (3) rationalization of the Christian vision of

97

the world.[1] With the first two, I believe, the Orthodox have usually not had difficulty. The third, of course, is another story. Were I to be bold enough to restate the three points, I would put them in two points by joining the first two and changing the language in the third. I would say that theological concern must occur in two ways: (1) speaking the truth of the Christian message; and (2) implementing that truth in the flesh of each new generation.

The "implementation" mentioned in the second point is, at once, the special task and the problem of pastoral theology.

Tension is Needed. Right from the start, it should be said that these two points are inextricably bound; one cannot implement without knowing—and understanding—*what* it is that must be implemented. Said in another way, a constant and creative "tension" must be maintained between *praxis* (practice) and *theory* if pastoral theology will be "done" properly. This I see as a crucial point to be understood; the words of this "tension" are *praxis* and *theory*, and *not* praxis and theology. The distinction *is* crucial because what is needed is a *theological praxis*, a phrase that has often been mistakenly thought of as self-disqualifying, but should never be so for the Orthodox.

Some explanation is obviously needed. It is not infrequent that competence in the praxis of the priesthood is thought to be solely a matter of proper attitude, technique, and style; it is an unlearnable calling of the heart, a vocation, which is coupled with an inexplicable quality called "charisma." While our ministry is such a calling of the heart, scholarship and "theology" are gifts of the intellect and will. Thus, *theological education* becomes solely a matter of *theoretical pursuit*. The "tension" between theory and praxis is lost and theology comes to *mean* theory.

This division, which begins with the division between *kardia* (heart) and *nous* (mind), cannot be accepted in the perspective of pastoral theology since the practice of theology and the practice of the ministry cannot be divided. The danger

[1]Julian N. Hartt, *Theological Method and Imagination* (New York: Seabury, 1977) 4f.

of this dichotomy is seen when a "transition" is made from the seminary graduate to the pastor: the assumption is made that the theological task—which was only "theory" in any case—is completed. Theological learning ceases so that the practice of the ministry can begin. This is obviously wrong, since the practice of the ministry must be the practice of theology.

Pastoral theology, then, sees a most important function of theological activity emerging both *out of* and *for the sake of* the ministry of the priesthood (of course, of both *kleros* and *laos*). The important point here is that the practice of the priesthood is itself an intrinsic theological activity since it is the "being in act" of theology.

In short, one cannot speak of theology and praxis as if they were different, but rather of *theological praxis.*

Proper Praxis against Reduction. Of what is this praxis comprised? If it is indeed a theological matter, how can we understand all that it involves? Here it is best for us to measure this question of praxis against two reductions.

In the first place, pastoral theology as a *subject* includes, but is not limited to, "counseling." Furthermore, it is not distinguished by any preference for a particular sociological, psychological, medical, etc., theory. It has a more comprehensive foundation than each of these and cannot be reduced to any. It does deal with communal and individual life and growth. It does deal with categories of faith, trust, despair, aging, dying, etc. It does deal with problems of marriage, of interpersonal dynamics, of family life. If in the praxis of the priesthood, the attempt is to deal with such aforementioned life categories, then all those factors, from the cultural environment to the political mood, from the theater to the last newspaper editorial, must be considered.[2] It is in this

---

[2]Here we must adopt the careful pattern of the Fathers, according to which "worldly study" (St. Basil) can sharpen the mind for the reception of higher knowledge, although like a bee, we must take only the honey (*Homily on Psalm 33*). St. John Chrysostom, in *How Parents Should Raise their Children*, and St. Gregory of Nyssa, in *The Life of Moses*, both maintain a guarded attitude toward "secular" learning (Greek philosophical and

context that the pastor must understand such sociological, psychological, medical, or otherwise, information for his *own* purposes of dealing with the problem. It will be his Orthodox Christian understanding of human life which will influence the decision about which of the options, gleaned from such information, can be applied to his proper praxis. Here we see that his theological conviction influences what he will say or do (or *not* say or do!) as he attempts to "make contact" with the real issues with which the people must live.

This, of course, is not the "safest" area in which to do theological work, but it is the job of the pastor and the task of pastoral theology; this is the "cutting edge" at which pastoral theology works, and it again shows that one must be solidly grounded in Orthodox theology to properly assure this "tension." Thus, the qualities—in themselves—of a psychologist, a sociologist, a medical doctor, or a social worker cannot deal with pastoral theology in the fulness with which I am describing it; it takes a man of theology, a man of the Church.

The second reduction is related to the first, but is nevertheless distinct: it is the reduction of theological praxis to *experience only*, i.e., the break in "tension" in which the *theory* in lost. The danger is that the scriptural and historic content of the faith may be lost in the pressure of concern about the present. *Memory* and *language* are here crucial and are part of the guarantors of the proper tension. As I am now referring to it, this memory and language can only be acquired by what the Fathers have called *apperception*, the consciousness or conscience (συνείδησις), i.e., the immediate or intuitive cognition and judgment, and must be a part of every Orthodox pastor's make-up.

Ray Anderson speaks of a "theological instinct" in *Theological Foundations for Ministry*[3] and comes close to my point regarding both the tension and consciousness in pas-

---

pagan thought): it can be of use, although *by itself* it will always fall short of the complete fulness of revelation in Christ.

[3]See his article "Toward a Theology of Ministry," in the collection he edited, *Theological Foundations for Ministry* (Grand Rapids, Mich.: Eerdmans, 1978).

toral theology. He speaks of this "instinct" in terms of a *paradigm coherence,* a *truthful presence,* and a *theological nerve.* I would like briefly to point to all three, but now in an Orthodox perspective.

Through *paradigm coherence* this instinct is rooted in the objective reality of God's own act in Christ and the Holy Spirit as a paradigm for the practice of the ministry; this of course includes both revelation and reconciliation. Here we see that instinct does not mean an acting out of whatever impulse happens to be present. Rather, this "instinct" means being rooted in and acting out of an informed mind and heart which is steeped in the wisdom of "the patriarchs, prophets, apostles, preachers, evangelists, martyrs, confessors, ascetics, and every righteous spirit made perfect in faith" (Liturgy of St. John Chrysostom).

By *truthful presence* (and especially, as he puts it, "rather than artful dodge"), what is meant is precisely what I referred to as "being in act." Here we are to remember Mark 2:27 and the words of Christ that "The Sabbath was made for man, not man for the Sabbath." This response of Jesus was an "instinctive" one which rested in the sense of presence that He brought to each situation. He countered the appeal to Moses by saying, "I say to you" (Matt. 19:9), and to those who appealed to Abraham, "Before Abraham was, I am" (John 8:58). Needless to say, the *truthful presence* must be conditioned by *responsibility* and *commitment,* i.e., it must be truthful.

By *theological nerve,* he means the courage to transform a *human situation* into a *theological task* (more on this later in the Orthodox model).

The reduction of pastoral theology to experience only requires the antidote of the presence of such an "instinct," which I call the consciousness of the priesthood.

Such a theological instinct, then, results from the scholarly knowledge of the revealed truth which, in turn, can interpret the concrete situation. Regarding this point, in my notes I have a quote by Schillebeeckx, the source of which I am honestly not sure: "theology is the critical self-consciousness of Christian praxis in the world and in the Church."

Both these reductions, then, must be guarded against if one is to protect the "tension" necessary for a proper pastoral theology, especially in the curriculum of Orthodox schools of theology.

Word of God and Human Act. But besides the problem of reduction, there are those who speak of "primacy" whenever the problem of *God's Word* and the *human life and act* intersect. Writers such as Karl Barth[4] and Helmut Thielicke,[5] writing under the title of "evangelical," give much attention to this question of "primacy." Looking with an Orthodox eye, it seems that in their concern for guarding against "Pelagianism" (which of course *is* a justifiable concern) they fall into the trap of Augustine's anthropology (rewritten, of course, in Luther, Calvin, etc.), of "predestinationism" and salvation by "faith alone." One cannot avoid seeing what such writers know as the difficulty of the Cartesian theology (Thielicke even labels it "Theology A") in which the existential "I," the human subject, is the basis for the act of theologizing. Such writers advocate that in such a circumstance (in the frame of Cartesian theology) the Word of God is not free to determine for *itself* the method of *knowing* itself; the human life and act provide the method, thus causing us to "appropriate" the Word. The Word of God, thus, must stand alone in its "primacy." It seems, then, to be "split" from the *true* engagement in the human life and act.

The Orthodox have to see this question of "primacy" as an artificial one. For anyone who reads the Fathers and understands the "synergist" truth of salvation, God's Word will not act without human will; divine grace and human act are *both* required. "We are fellow-workers [συνεργοὶ] with God" (1 Cor. 3:9). Such writers confuse the *crucial* question with the *methodological* one, and this is what makes "primacy," in this case, artificial. For the Orthodox it is not "which comes first," i.e., "primacy"—God's grace and human

[4]In his *Evangelical Theology* (New York: Holt, Rinehart and Winston, 1963) 1-12, 15-19.

[5]In his *Evangelical Faith* 1 (Grand Rapids, Mich.: Eerdmans, 1974) 129-60, 163-205.

will *are* unequal (the *crucial* question)—but *both* *are* *required* (the methodological question). What God has done and always does is immeasurably more prominent than what man does, but the cooperation of two unequal forces is still necessary. The Orthodox have never confused the question of "importance" with "necessity," which is to say "primacy" with "cooperation." The Fathers, never forgetting who was who, who was the Creator and the created, the immutable and the changeable, the absolute and the relative, really did not seem to have this problem!

In terms of pastoral theology, then, the Orthodox know that, although the source of growth and change in human life and act is *ad extra*, the response is nevertheless *ad intra*. A *personal* (and here the word "personal" is crucial) relationship in which God encounters a concrete man, in a specific situation in time and space, constitutes a proper synergy. The kerygma must constantly engage life as it is—what is, in a sense, *already there*—or else it remains outside and non-dialectical.

Seeing the divine Word and human life and act in such a dynamic is the only attitude with which Orthodox can speak of both *fides quaerens intellectum* ("faith seeking understanding") and *credo ut intelligam* ("I believe in order to understand"). Pastoral theology sees "theology" in this way, and this is the *only* way in which St. Paul speaks of λογικὴ λατρεία, a "reasonable service" (Rom. 12:1).

An Orthodox Model

But if the problem is one of maintaining this constant and creative "tension," the outcome of which is a veritable *theological praxis*, what kind of Orthodox model can be seen? How can this problem inform one such Orthodox model? How can we guard against reduction?

To accomplish the explication of such an Orthodox model, I would like to utilize various graphic schemes which I believe will help to clarify at a glance how I see pastoral theology in the Orthodox curriculum.

Dynamics of Orthodox Pastoral Theology. I would like to begin explaining the dynamic of pastoral theology in an Orthodox model by reiterating that it is not only "counseling" (which usually occurs when things go wrong, e.g., in crises). It *is* that, but more. The dynamic is centered around St. Irenaeus' words: "The glory of God is man most fully alive, and the life of man is the vision of God" (*Adversus haereses*, 4, 20, 6). This "being alive," of course, is more than mere existing, more than biologic living; it is being "alive unto God through Jesus Christ." Because the task is man being "fully alive," the dynamic of pastoral theology calls to mind such aspects as man's *being, experience, circumstance, identity, relationship, growth,* etc.

These aspects of man's life were affected by the incarnation, and in the deepest sense, then, the basis of pastoral theology rests in the theological dynamic of the incarnation. My belief is that we best grasp the meaning of the incarnation when we *experience* the truth that in Christ, God placed Himself in the world, even sharing and experiencing the debasement of the human condition, and ultimately the final humiliation: death. "Though He was in the form of God, He did not deem equality with God something to be grasped at. Rather, He emptied Himself and took the form of a slave being born in the likeness of man" (Phil. 2:6-7). Or, said more simply, "The *Logos* became flesh and dwelt among us" (Prologue of St. John).

We best realize what this can *mean* for our human experience when we read the Gospels and see in life what Jesus saw there. Ultimately, the dynamic of pastoral theology as a *subject* is a "reawakening" of this incarnational truth— not as a metaphysic, not as an alembic of theological investigation, but as a truth that really does engage the human experience. The accomplishment of this shows the true raison d'être of pastoral theology as a subject, and not as an addendum to any other area of the curriculum.

Because this task is as it is, it is only one who is doing *this* praxis who is the true "therapist." No one should be too shocked to hear my language here, since it is a matter of proper philology. The word "therapist" comes from the ancient θεράπων, for "Godly servant" or, rather, θεραπεία Θεοῦ. The Church, which had this term wrestled from her by secular psychology (which may hardly have anything to do with God), must now reclaim it as her own. This task of pastoral theology again helps to show the true etymology of this term as rightly belonging in the Church.

At this point, then, I would like to present the following diagram, which, along with the explanation to follow, can show more exactly the scheme of incarnational dynamics in pastoral theology, and can explain the synthesis of praxis and theory, particularly as it relates to the pedagogical task of the Orthodox seminary curriculum.

SCHEME OF PASTORAL DYNAMICS

1° — *tension* — 2° — ➤		THERAPEUTIC ➤ SCREEN	GROWTH SCREEN
Scripture		*Healing* • Anointing	
Liturgy		• Exorcising *Sustaining*	Synergy
Doctrine		⊙ Preservation	
Patristics	Pastoral Theology	• Consolation *Guidance*	Theosis
Ethics		• Advice • Listening	
Tradition		*Reconciliation* • Forgiveness • Discipline	Telos

Naturally Orthodox pastors and seminarians will be grounded in a particular foundation. These elements will be the first degree (1°) and will be comprised of such subjects as Scripture, liturgy, doctrine, etc. Pastoral theology is built upon this foundation, maintaining the aforementioned "tension." It is at the second degree (2°) where the implementation or the praxis occurs, i.e., where one is to be transparent to this foundation (and ultimately, of course, thereby transparent to Christ).

At the *second degree*, however, something is to happen in which the theological imperatives of the foundation can be transmitted. Said simply, praxis must past through a "screen" or "filter" of a sort. The screen has four particular "therapeutic" (based on the previous *therapon*-as-Godly-servant) aspects of pastoral care. I have in a sense, "Orthodoxized" these aspects from Clebsh and Jaekle's *Pastoral Care in Historical Perspective.*[6] They are *healing, sustaining, guiding,* and *reconciling.* I would like now to consider each in the perspective of what I have hitherto presented.

Healing has been expressed in the Orthodox Church by *anointing* and *exorcising.* It deals with *overcoming,* e.g., overcoming "Satan and all his angels, all his works, all his service and all his pride." It refers to restoring the person to wholeness (ὅλος). In terms of pastoral praxis, when such healing occurs in the lives of persons, e.g., in a crisis situation, it is not just returning him to where he was before his crisis, but *beyond* his previous condition. The crisis, in other words, is *used to grow.* The person is to be integrated on a higher spiritual level than he previously experienced. Even a terminal illness can be a gain when one can discover his generic human limitation, i.e., the consciousness of his own being before God. This is what Berdyaev perhaps meant when he said "consciousness *is* pain."[7] Is there any *real* growth without such pain?

Sacramentally, this healing is expressed and realized in anointing and exorcising, along with which counseling of the deepest kind is needed.

Sustaining has been expressed in terms such as *preservation* and *consolation.* Here we see endurance; this is Job, or our Lord Himself. In our praxis, a person must be helped to endure the hurt or pain of a circumstance and even to interpret it in such a way as to *transcend* it. In this way he can be *restored* to his *status quo ante,* i.e., to the state at which

[6] William A. Clebsh and Charles R. Jaekle, *Pastoral Care in Historical Perspective* (Englewood Cliffs, N. J.: Prentice-Hall, 1964).

[7] Nicholas Berdyaev, *The Destiny of Man* (New York: Harper and Row, 1960) 39. "Consciousness is born in pain and suffering. Consciousness *is* pain, and loss of consciousness appears to us as the cessation of pain. Dostoevsky says that suffering is the only cause of consciousness."

he was before his suffering. This is especially required when confronted with the dying and grieving.

Guiding, expressed as *advice* and *listening*, has to do with *direction*. This is the area of the *staretz* and the father confessor. In our praxis, one comes to us confused and not able to make a choice. He is torn, ambivalent, between alternative courses of thought and action in which not everything is black and white to him. Here is where the "tension" is needed in which those fundamental aspects of the first degree are needed along with an applicable understanding of the human situation.

Reconciliation we know as *forgiveness* and *discipline*. Here enters the reality of "the fall" in our lives, in which restoration and return is required, in terms of reestablishing broken relationships and communion. Here also is ἐπιτίμησις as rebuke, and confession as "entrance."

These four aspects of this "screen" again remind us that pastoral theology is pastoral *and* theological, and cannot be reduced to medicine, teaching, counseling, etc.

Periodization of Pastoral Theology. How has the Church in history dealt with the "people of God" in such a way that the "tension" has been maintained? How has she been faithful to both the praxis and the theory, to the "being in act" of theology? How has she continuously "incarnated" the faith vis-à-vis the life-situation as it existed in each epoch?

In order to at least partially answer such a question, it would be necessary to give some scheme of *periodization* of pastoral theology. This will give us some idea of where we have been, where we are, and even the possibility of where we must go.[8] For the sake of continuity, each era we discuss will be measured against the "screen" in our pastoral dynamic scheme, i.e., of healing, sustaining, guidance, and reconciliation.

The era of *primitive Christianity*, from the time of our

[8] I do realize here that, depending on one's starting point and bias, many eras in history can be marked. For my immediate purposes, I use the following four generalized eras to put pastoral theology into an Orthodox historical perspective.

Lord's life, death, and resurrection in history to about
A.D. 180, was marked by the *sustaining* (second on the
"screen") of souls through the vicissitudes of life in this
world since they felt the *parousia* was upon them. It was the
"second coming" which galvanized all pastoral care. This
pervasive attitude of waiting for the Lord was no problem
until the advent of concern for *sin after baptism*; they had
time to sin and perhaps the *parousia* was not coming "in
their time." Something now had to be said about dealing with
postbaptismal sin—*penance*—and the angel of penance in the
form of a shepherd: the *Shepherd of Hermas* is written. In
a sense, this closes this primitive period of pastoral care as
sustaining.

In the *persecution era*, roughly from 180 to 306 (the end
of Diocletian's reign), the pastoral concern centered around
reconciliation (fourth on the "screen"). Here we come upon
the problem of the "lapsed" and St. Cyprian. How were the
lapsed to be reconciled? Was the Church to follow the rigorist
way of Tertullian, Novatian, and Hippolytus, or go the way
of Cyprian, who felt that they must be integrated into full
communion even if various *epitimiai* and penalties are needed?

In the era of *Christian culture*, after Christianity became
the legal faith of the state, the Church suddenly found herself providing a new principle for unity in the Roman empire.
Beginning with Constantine in the early fourth century and
down through the Golden Age of Justinian, Christianity became the unifying agent and the judge—and of course, the
accuser. Theodosius' Edict of Thessalonica in 380 said that
now church "membership" was coterminus with citizenship.
In this period we have, among others, Chrysostom accusing
clergy and Eudoxia in Constantinople, the Cappadocians defending against heretics, and monasticism blossoming forth
as a reaction to the world. The concern was *guiding* (third
on the "screen") the people of God who must live in the
new danger of "this world."

For me there could be no other title for the time follow-
ing the "era of Christian culture" than the era of *post-
Christian culture*. Marked by the Enlightenment and the
Renaissance, it involves technology, individualism, pluralism,

etc., all of which could probably be labeled "secularism," which, in a sense, "backfired" in the face of Christianity. Of course, given all the various trends, movements, styles, etc., which could probably be subtitles of this era, this is in general still our age. It involves all four areas on our pastoral screen.

The Growth Screen. The second screen in our pastoral dynamic scheme we have labeled a growth screen. This I believe is the most neglected area of pastoral care. All that will be said here—as indicated by the theological "process" terms of growth, i.e., *synergy, theosis,* and *telos*—is that it deals with modes of *moving people on* in their growth "into Christ."

More particularly, *baptism* and *marriage* are examples. Baptism must be looked at as an expansive and ongoing *process*, rather than an isolated *event*. In a pastoral perspective, whenever that process of growth gets stifled (for whatever reason!), whenever κοινωνία and ἀγάπη are blocked, it is the pastor's responsibility to help discover and remove such blocks in order to further "cooperate" with God's evercoming energy.

In marriage, event must also surrender to process—or rather, the event of marriage must *lead* to a process of growing together and into Christ. It is not enough to "crown them with glory and honor" and now our jobs are completed! It is time that the Orthodox discover that it is precisely the one who *does* crown them, who prays for the union in which "you shall see your children's children and peace in Israel," and *not* the secular shrink, who is responsible. Which Orthodox pastor has not seen married persons excommunicated from each other and God because they find themselves on two islands with no way to reach other!

There are, of course, other aspects of this "growth screen" through which pastoral theology must pass, e.g., not only dealing with *crises* in growth, but in providing ways for that growth process to happen *before and even without* a crisis. Is it enough to pick up a person after he has fallen off a cliff, or can we help him before he gets to the edge?

In these ways, and many more, this growth screen indicates that the Orthodox pastor is not a mere *administrator*. Nor is he to serve Liturgy and preach as a robot. The Church does not exist merely to exist, but to provide a way, indeed it *is* the very way, of bringing God and man together and thus continuously establishing the Kingdom of God which is both here and waited for. In a pastoral perspective, then, speaking of growth *process* instead of *event* (which *begins* and *is part* of the continual process) is the only way to realize what the sacraments mean as a continual εἴσοδος (entrance); it is the realization and actualization of "liturgy after Liturgy," as pastoral theology must see it.

Some Special Concerns of Pastoral Theology. There are some special concerns with which we are faced in the contemporary scheme of things. These concerns must be considered if we are to see pastoral theology in its fulness and with the proper "tension." I would like to posit three such special concerns.

(1) The *fulness of concern in itself* can be shown in the following diagram:

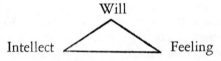

Will

Intellect   Feeling

These three "faculties," each of which are part of the spiritual life, must be considered by pastoral theology. They must be brought into one harmonious wholeness in which all three are properly activated in the life of the person. The mind, for example, must judge the desirability of acting upon certain emotions, according to the dictates of our will. (Heart is brought into the mind and vice-versa.)

Any dysfunction of will, intellect, or feeling (emotion) must be dealt with by one doing his pastoral work. Always and only, such work is to be done within the "tension" of praxis and theory.[9]

---

[9]We are aware here of the teaching of *apatheia*, but it is an area that requires special attention and with which the pastor will seldom, if at all, have to deal in the contemporary "in-the-world" situation.

(2) There is a *wisdom* necessary when pastoral theology comes to deal with elements of *psychology*. These are: (a) being aware of any easy alliance with a specific system or "school" of academic psychology; (b) remaining *open* to important insights of growth and development which can be brought into the service of the pastoral task; (c) being aware of *vocabulary* which describes *human trouble*—it is the best way to help and, if need be, to transcend that vocabulary; and (d) maintaining a reverence for the historic function of pastoral theology.

(3) What *practically* is the composition of pastoral theology? I see this as a special concern, and I have diagrammed it in the following way, according to the two predominate sources of *attitude* and *skill*. Unlike many others who develop an "either-or" problem between these two sources, I see *attitude* and *skill* as both needed.

Attitude is:	Skill is:
• Spontaneous	• Discipline
• Art	• Direction
• Creative	• Vision
• Existential	• Language (Silence)

We develop *attitude* by attempting "to get on the inside" of the phenomenon (e.g., suffering, aging, dying, etc.) or, put in another way, understanding the phenomenon as a *subject* in itself. This sensitizes us to that with which the person is living, and to what his problem really is. Attitude is best captured by terms such as spontaneous, creative, art, existential, etc.

We develop *skill* by studying how one can *respond* to that phenomenon, both as a helping pastor and as the person living with the phenomenon. Skill is best captured by terms such as discipline, direction, vision, language, etc.

If pastoral theology is to develop as a subject unto itself in Orthodoxy, it will take discipline and reading, sharing and exploring, all of which is needed to develop *both* attitude and skill.

The Realization of Preparing for Pastoral Theology

Having now considered first, the general problem, and second, the Orthodox model and concerns of pastoral theology, one naturally must ask, "How then can pastoral theology be realized as a taught subject?" Here we come across: (1) reading and reporting of topical areas; (2) theological reflection of "lived experience"; and (3) applied theology. Of course, varying opinions and styles abound regarding this "how," but I believe that with these three items we arrive at the best *modus operandi* for the Orthodox seminary curriculum.

(1) *Reading and reporting on the topical areas,* e.g., marriage, sexuality, aging, etc., could comprise a weekly class. Intense reading during the week in preparation for the class should be done in Scripture, the Fathers, and contemporary literature. Needless to say, the contemporary literature must be read not to accept all that is written there, but to see what valuable information can be gleaned from it, and what information cannot be accepted (and *why!*) in an Orthodox perspective. After all, this is the "scrimmage line"!

(2) *Theological reflection* must be done in conjunction with the "lived experience," e.g., in the field work of the seminarian. It is an attempt at "thinking" theologically as issues and experiences arise in their field assignment. This forces their theological and foundational education to inform, challenge, disrupt and/or confirm life experiences. Such *theological reflection* can be held in scheduled sessions where groups of students doing "field work" can come together and share in a *guided* discussion. Each can be assigned a reflection session, which will include three distinct steps: (a) *reviewing*—what are the basic facts and conditions of the situation, e.g., in the church school, hospital, home of the grieving, etc.; (b) *exploring*—what are the interpersonal relationships and feelings involved, etc.; and (c) *reflecting*—what are the theological issues and how do they relate the resources of the Church and their own persons to the praxis of the circumstances.

(3) All of pastoral theology, of course, is *"applied"* the-

ology, but what is meant in this title is a style of education in which particular "case studies" are brought into a class situation. These case studies can carry the student into a contemporary life situation, which can extend from problems of organ transplantation to addiction, family relations, adolescence, etc., each of which we are confronted with more and more and must meet with our best theological acumen.

These, then, are some of the sources which can be utilized in meeting the challenge of teaching pastoral theology in an Orthodox curriculum.

CHAPTER 7

THE SYNTHESIS IN
A SACRED TENSION

We may know the human only when we are confronted with the divine. We may know the temporal only when we ponder the eternal. And we may know the depth of the valley only when we look at the peak of the mountain. We are sick and paralyzed by fear and will never be healed without a true encounter with Christ.

Metropolitan Philip

Demetrios Constantelos, Professor of Church History at Brockton State College, has prepared this article from a presentation originally given at Duquesne University in Pittsburgh in August 1979. A man so often known to honestly "speak his mind," the author writes of the Christian and Orthodox synthesis as it is focused around the "single event" which stands between the ancient Greco-Roman civilization and the early Christian centuries. His claim, thus, is a simple one: humanity was always searching for God, and this search is completed in the event of the incarnation. Fr. Constantelos establishes the fact that not every person has the same perception of God's act in history, but that through the Church and her experience, these varying perceptions are bound into a oneness and unity. In establishing this truth, the author demonstrates that the two factors of Christian consciousness, love (ἀγάπη) and faith (πίστις), as they engage the existing Spirit of God, serve as the basis for the establishment of a Christian culture as "an organic part of the whole society."

J. J. A.

Varying Encounters with God in the Christian Life

by

DEMETRIOS CONSTANTELOS

From its very inception, the Christian life was perceived as having a novel style, with a different appreciation and a new understanding of the meaning of life. One of the early Christian protagonists emphasized that "if anyone is in Christ, he is a new creation" (2 Cor. 5:17). But what is the verdict of history? Did Christ introduce a new kind of life, and how varied is the life in Christ? Is it possible that Christians claim too much as their own?

From a historical perspective, Christ indeed introduced a new era, a new order, and a new style of life. History, to be sure, is continuous—we only divide it into chronological periods for conventional and practical purposes. Nevertheless, there are several personalities and certain events in history that provide some periods with an integrity or a completeness of their own. Such periods, for example, are the Mycenaean or Homeric age or the time of Pericles, and such is the Greco-Roman period as a whole. But a single event stands between ancient Greco-Roman civilization and the Christian centuries of the Greek East and the Latin West: the God-made-man event, i.e., the incarnation of Christ. Indeed, there is justification for the division of history into the "before Christ" and the *anno Domini* eras.

Some classical scholars believe that Christianity introduced nothing new, no values that did not exist in Greco-Roman civilization. But surely Christ was revolutionary when He made the daring claim that "I am the way, the truth, and the life" (John 14:6). "No man ever spoke like this man" (John 7:46), people used to say. He was revolutionary when He said, "A new commandment I give to you, that you love one another, even as I have loved you, you must also love one another" (John 13:34).

There is a principle that the simplest explanation of phenomena consistent with the available facts is usually the most scientifically correct. For example, when Copernicus dispensed with the complex Ptolemaic system of cycles and epicycles by setting the sun at the center of the universe, it was a scientific achievement, and when Newton was able to incorporate Kepler's laws of motion under the single law of gravitation, it was likewise a scientific advancement.

Faith and Agape

Something very similar applies in the sphere of religion and ethics. The human mind seeks a single principle of origins and a single principle of ethics. Thus, amidst the multitude of sects, cults, divinities, and the pantheon of Greco-Roman antiquity, humanity was searching for one God. Christ claimed to be the Son of God, God incarnate, who assumed humanity in order to deify the human. He appeared to many as the fulfillment of the aspirations and gropings of the ancient world. On the other hand, His teaching of the new commandment of *agape* reduced all ethical principles to one single dynamic. In the last analysis, it was faith in the risen Christ and the commandment of *agape* that served as the two major factors in spreading Christianity about the Roman empire, and that explains why Christianity succeeded where other religions failed. Whereas Greco-Roman religion was perplexed and confused and Judaism remained a particularistic tribal faith or culture, Christianity transcended race, color, and creed, and slowly but steadily transformed the peoples and societies in what we call today the western tradition.

Transformation then, *metamorphosis*, μετάνοια, or complete change of mind and heart to conform to the will of God, is the essence of the life in Christ. Nevertheless, during the formative years of mainstream Christianity, Christians experienced varying encounters with both God and the secular world. Christianity and Greco-Roman culture engaged in vital and mutual interactions. The ultimate result of those interactions was that Christianity did not divorce itself from secular culture but became an organic part of the whole society. Its dissemination in Greek culture and thought did not diminish its power and influence, but, to be sure, the perils of its translation from a particularistic creed into a universal religion were very real. "But the risk was worth taking, even though it was fraught with many disasters. Of course it was worthwhile, otherwise Gentile Christianity [i.e., Greek Christianity] would have perished as Jewish Christianity did," in the words of an evangelical theologian.[1] Early Christian thinkers such as Justin the Martyr, Clement and Origen of Alexandria, and many more showed that the risk of translating the gospel as thoroughly as Justin did into other thought forms was a very worthwhile procedure. "They used the Greek epics; they used the Homeric myths, and also Stoic and Epicurean philosophy when it suited them. . . . Anything in Greek thought that would help his listeners to lay hold of the wonder and the reality of the resurrection was good enough for Clement [of Rome]. And this is the characteristic aim which the Greek exponents of the gospel set themselves: to embody biblical doctrine in culture forms which would be acceptable in their society."[2] Thus the "good news" was expressed in terms comprehensible both to individuals and to nations.

Few can doubt the transforming powers of the Christian faith. It was a personal encounter with Christ that changed a fanatic persecutor like Saul (Acts 8:1-3) into a vigorous missionary of love renamed Paul (Acts 9:1-19); it was faith in Christ that changed a perplexed and searching youth named

---

[1]Michael Green, *Evangelism in the Early Church* (Grand Rapids, Mich.: Eerdmans, 1975) 141.

[2]Ibid., p. 142.

Augustine into a major thinker and Christian intellectual;[3] it was faith in Christ that transformed a professional prostitute like Mary the Egyptian into an honored saint. Faith in Christ has given strength to criminals, drug addicts, and thieves to overcome their habits and has led some to tear out a long-cherished hate from their hearts and become apostles of love.

But the "new life in Christ" means more than the fruits of the Holy Spirit as St. Paul describes them (Gal. 5:22-23). It means a certainty that the individual lives ever in the presence of God, that nothing else is more desirable to the individual than a perpetual relationship with the Creator. A new life in Christ means a constant struggle with God, for God, and about God; a love affair between the divine and the human with its ups and downs, its crises and consummations.

A Christian does not live for himself. "If we live, we live for the Lord, and if we die, we die for the Lord; so . . . whether we live or whether we die, we are the Lord's" (Rom. 14:8). A life in Christ presupposes belief in Christ's living presence as a constant dynamic in one's very being. There is no descent or ascent, there is no outpouring from on high, though these terms may be used as metaphors and symbols. There is, however, an ever-present awareness, an ever-vivid consciousness that this is God's world and God is everywhere and fills all things, including the human being. The Kingdom of God may be a metaphysical reality, but it has its beginning here on earth. "The Kingdom of God is within you," as the Master said (Luke 17:21).

But God's presence in history is perceived differently by different people. The *sacred tension* between the Spirit of God and the spirit of man is not of the same intensity in every person. The "new life" that Christ introduced can be lived in diverse ways and in different degrees. There is neither your way nor my way. There are several ways under the aegis and guidance of the same Spirit. The Holy Spirit, the producer of the new fruits, is not an extraterrestrial power that out-

[3]See Augustine's *Confessions* 1:1: "O Lord . . . you have created us for yourself, and our hearts are restless till they find rest in you."

pours itself at certain times and places. The Holy Spirit is of the same essence as the Father and the Son and together with Father and Son is present everywhere and at all times. One participates in the Spirit in one's daily existence and by participation is made "sharer in the divine nature" (2 Pet. 1:4). It is not whether the Spirit of God grants gifts (charismata) but whether one is conscious of the presence of the gifts and appropriates and cultivates them. The difference in spirituality among the faithful is a difference in degree, in personal awareness, in intensity, and in consciousness.

There are different styles of Christian life because God has distributed different talents to His people. St. Paul exhorted the faithful to think of themselves according to the measure of faith that God assigned to them; they are members of the same organism, but all Christians do not have the same functions. Their life in Christ assumes the character that corresponds to their talents, to their inclinations, and to their charismata. "Having gifts that differ according to the grace given to us, let us use them: he who serves, in serving; he who teaches, in his teaching; he who exhorts, in his exhortation; he who contributes, in liberality; he who gives aid, with zeal; he who does acts of mercy, with cheerfulness" (Rom. 12:6-8). Elsewhere St. Paul acknowledged that not everyone could live as he lived because "each has his own special gift from God, one of one kind and one of another" (1 Cor. 7:7). What has been important in the history of the Church is that each one should employ his or her charisma for self-edification as well as for the benefit of the Christian community. St. Peter advised: "as each has received a gift, employ it for one another, as good stewards of God's varied grace" (1 Pet. 4:10).

The Experience of the Historical Church

But what is the experience of the Christian community—the Church in history? Life in Christ in history and tradition presupposes a life in full agreement with the precepts of Holy Scripture and the theology of the liturgy. Every style and every aspect of the new life must have its roots in the gospel and should derive its inspiration from the example of Christ.

The early Christian community possessed the moral earnestness and authoritative teachings handed down by Christ and His Apostles. The faithful, whether of the East or of the West, displayed a marked sense of vocation, a glow of certainty, a joy difficult to hide, a love that prompted non-Christians to comment "look how much they love each other." In a decaying and confused world like that of late antiquity, Christians possessed a mind that expressed itself in terms of the variety of charismata and vocations in the belief that God's Spirit is present in history—in Scripture reading and in prayer, in liturgy and in sacrament, in monastic withdrawal and in social involvement, in teaching and exhortation, in evangelism and prophecy, in witnessing and martyrdom. Thus, the influence of Christ must be seen in proportion to an individual's faith under the given circumstances.

The experience of "new life" has persisted throughout the centuries. From time to time in the Orthodox tradition and history the "new life" has assumed different dimensions. Sometimes it appears dormant, sometimes very active. Some of its manifestations have been spectacular and highly emotional; other manifestations have appeared more intellectual and theological; still others more mystical and ethical. Some Christians believed and still believe that the best and most characteristic fruit of the new life in Christ is a spiritual and moral rebirth, with "love, joy, peace, long-suffering, kindness, gentleness, meekness, self-control" (Gal. 5:22-23). Without a doubt, these principles were and are the fundamentals of the life in Christ. Nevertheless, faith in the person of Christ remained the basis of the impulse that gave rise to many movements within and without the Christian ecclesia. Even though many ideas and practices were derived from other religions and schools of thought—elements from Judaism and Greek philosophies, national prejudices and characteristics, experiences and personal beliefs peculiar to outstanding Christians such as St. Paul, Marcion, Montanus, or Augustine—most of these early types of Christianity accorded Christ a primary place.

St. Anthony, for example, the outstanding leader and exponent of the monastic style of the "new life," was led to take the decisive step of his life by the passage in the Gospel in which Christ commanded the rich ruler to sell what he had and give it to the poor. For Anthony and numerous other Christians after the third century, life in Christ meant to depart to the desert, to the monastery or the convent, where one could be preoccupied with one thing only and one service: to be in constant contemplation of God. The ideal of monasticism was not so much a rejection of the world as it was the desire to achieve spiritual perfection. But monasticism, too, was not one-sided, uniform, or monolithic. Some sought in *askesis* and *theoria* to achieve the highest good, others to serve the humble and the discarded in the alleys and streets of a city's slums. For example, Eulogius, a wealthy and educated man of Alexandria, distributed his possessions to the poor and to charitable concerns, keeping for himself only the essentials. While wandering through the agora of Alexandria, he noticed a man crippled and mutilated in his hands and feet. As if this were not enough, the mutilated man suffered also from an active case of leprosy. Eulogius, in his belief that serving an indigent person was serving Christ, took the leper into his own home, under his own roof, nursing and washing him regularly for nearly fifteen years.[4]

Eulogius was not an exception. In the long history and tradition of the Church there have been many who have experienced the impact of the Holy Spirit and have produced different fruits. They are witnesses who go by different names and under different categories—prophets and apostles, saints and fathers, martyrs and wonderworkers, laymen and monks, priests and bishops—people of all walks of life. People like Basil and Gregory the Cappadocians, John Eleemon of Alexandria, and Philaretus of Pontus expressed their life in Christ not only in prayer or theological teachings and writings but also in care for the sick and the poor: in their efforts to

[4]For Eulogius and other saints who translated their faith into action, see my book, *Byzantine Philanthropy and Social Welfare* (New Brunswick, N. J.: Rutgers Byzantine Series, 1968) 67-110.

build hospitals, leprosaria, homes for the elderly and orphans.[5] In imitation of their Master they went about doing good. Others, such as Chrysostom and Athanasius I of Constantinople, spent much of their lives seeking ways to bridge the gap between social classes, between the rich and the poor; whereas persons like Photius and Nicholas Mysticus exerted many efforts to establish peace between nations. Several others, such as Eustathius of Sebastea, Justinian's wife Theodora, Philotheus of Heraclea, and Andronicus of Berrhoia, combated slavery, prostitution, and other iniquities.[6] A few, including Maximus the Confessor, Theodore the Studite, and Patriarch Arsenius, struggled against political corruption and abuse of power.

Many well-known saints and numerous anonymous heroes of the faith such as Eulogius have gone to repulsive slums of large cities, including Antioch, Alexandria, Ancyra, Constantinople, Athens, St. Petersburg, and Bucharest, in order to bring light and hope to the destitute. Many scores of believers, people like the obscure monk Telemachus, who sacrificed himself in order to stop the inhuman gladiatorial games, Cosmas of Aetolia, Philotheus of Athens, and more than one hundred seventy other neomartyrs viewed their life in Christ as a task to bear witness to and to defend their faith and offer the supreme sacrifice on its behalf.[7] Orthodox history and tradition are filled with illustrations of men and women who bore witness to their faith and life in Christ in different ways. And Christ was the basis of their vision, their life was Christocentric.

Conclusion: Heresy and Orthodox Catholicity

Nevertheless, the history of Christianity illustrates that some individuals and some groups of people not only re-

[5]Ibid., pp. 152-276.

[6]I discuss the philanthropic activity of several Church Fathers of the late Byzantine world in my forthcoming book, Byzantine Society and Philanthropy: From the Fourth Crusade through the Fall.

[7]See Ioannes M. Perantones, Λεξικὸν τῶν Νεομαρτύρων, 3 vols. (Athens, 1972).

sponded differently to the teachings of Christ, but in their excessive and misguided zeal went astray, thus introducing schisms, heresies, and aberrations. Before five centuries of the Christian era were out, there were some eighty movements or groups that professed allegiance to Christ in unorthodox ways—Montanists, members of an apocalyptic movement that claimed a monopoly of spirituality, prophecy, and religious enthusiasm; Marcionites, who, while stressing love as the absolute standard of the gospel, excluded biblical law altogether; Donatists, the fourth-century rigorists who self-righteously viewed themselves as the only true members of the Church. And there were the Novatians, Arians, Nestorians, Monophysites, Eunomians, Nazarites, Samosatenians, and many more.[8] By the end of the same period, mainstream or catholic-orthodox Christianity emerged purified through synods and councils, debates and conflicts, human reason and divine inspiration. The emergence of splinter groups, heresies, and cults had been predicted by Jesus Himself, who had prayed for the unity of His community (John 17:11).

But unity in catholic-orthodox Christianity did *not* mean uniformity. Throughout the history of the Orthodox Church we observe several preferences and choices, many forms of devotion, and several ways of spiritual life. Evangelical zeal and charismatic fervor, deep mysticism and sacramental life, the simple prayer of Jesus and the profound prayers of Basil or Symeon the New Theologian, the simple spiritual wisdom of the desert fathers and the highly intellectualized thought of several Fathers and teachers of the Church, the pietistic and moralistic style of modern movements—every one and all have a place within the embrace of the Orthodox Church. No one movement has a monopoly on spirituality. Life in Christ has many dimensions, all of which, however unequal, supplement each other.

In its history, doctrine, worship, and religious culture, the Orthodox Church is like a beautiful mosaic, a whole icon, yet an icon made of many polychrome tesserae. A tessera by

[8]Epiphanius of Cyprus, *Panarion*, in Karl Hall, ed., *Epiphanius Ancoratus und Panarion* 1-3 (Leipzig, 1915, 1922, 1933). Epiphanius enumerates sixty Christian heresies and schisms. See his *Ancoratus* 12 and 13.

itself, detached or fallen off from the icon, loses much of its brilliance and its value. It is within the mosaic that it recovers its full value. Like tesserae, movements, persons, and even spiritual experiences achieve their full potential within the community—the Church. Under the aegis of the Church, charismatic movements and persons not only realize their charismata, but contribute to "the building up of the body of Christ" (Eph. 4:12).

CHAPTER 8

A SYNTHESIS OF CHRISTOLOGY AND ETHICS

How can the Church be faithful to her Master if she becomes stagnant, indifferent and satisfied within her four walls? If one reads the life of our Lord in the Gospels, he will find that He was the perfect missionary. "And He went about all Galilee, teaching in the synagogues and preaching the gospel of the Kingdom, and healing every disease and every infirmity among the people."

Metropolitan Philip

Professor Veselin Kesich, a member of the Serbian Orthodox Church and longtime Professor of New Testament at St. Vladimir's Seminary, uses 1 Peter to synthesize "Christological, ethical, and pastoral teachings, each as part of the one undivided whole." This old and true "friend" of so many young seminarians over his many teaching years, is careful to insure that these teachings are actually rooted in a solid doctrinal and unified basis. In order to demonstrate these points, the author takes the reader into the world of the Christians in the diaspora, scattered throughout Asia Minor. He first substantiates the validity and integrity of this epistle, then demonstrates that its contents, e.g., persecution, baptism, hope, etc., but especially election, serve as a true synthesis of Christian belief.

J. J. A.

1 Peter and the Doctrines of Primitive Christianity

by

Veselin Kesich

Among the earliest Christian documents a special place belongs to a letter of five short chapters known in the canon of the New Testament as 1 Peter. Both its themes and the creative way they are presented make this letter one of the most attractive as well as revealing of Christian writings. Neglected for a period of time by modern exegetes, the epistle is now being restored to its rightful place as a document of singular importance for a proper understanding of primitive Christian beliefs and practices. If only this short treatise remained to us, we would still have evidence of the essential elements of early Christological and ethical teachings.

The First Epistle of Peter is a complex piece of writing. It combines Christological, ethical, and pastoral teachings presented as one undivided whole. Its Christology appears universal in its implication, and its ethical teaching is far from exclusive. The love it presents knows no limits; it is extended to all, including pagan magistrates. Christians are called "to do good" to all without exception. And the pastoral duties the epistle commends, like its moral exhortations, come from its doctrinal teachings.

In order to appreciate the intentions of the author, the reasons for his writing, and the insights that he offered about the plight of the Christians to whom the letter was addressed, we must enter the world of primitive Christianity. This letter in turn informs us about the Christological and ethical teachings of this early Christian period. In this paper we shall proceed from a consideration of the structure and authorship of the epistle to a discussion of its Christological and ethical content.

The Question of Structure

Only recently have some biblical exegetes begun to consider this rich epistle as one of the major sources for our knowledge of the first Christian generation. Among the reasons for this neglect were two important ones: the prevailing view about the structure of the epistle, and the question of its authorship. The epistle was regarded either as a homily or as a composite work and not as a genuine letter, and its author was assumed to have written it in the second century, far removed from the time of the Apostle Peter. These two basic assumptions influenced the evaluation of the epistle itself. In the last few decades, however, certain scholars have seriously challenged these views of the structure of the epistle, as well as the problem of its authorship, and they have proposed new solutions, with new insights into its nature. They regard the letter as a genuine epistle written in the first century, during the time of Peter or else soon after his death.

The presence of Pauline ideas in the epistle was for some the cause of the most serious objections to Peter's authorship. The well-known Pauline expression "in Christ" is found in 1 Peter (3:16; 5:10, 14), and similarities with ideas expressed in Paul's letters have been detected in several other passages of 1 Peter. Was this a literary borrowing? Did Peter know of the Pauline letters?

In answer to these arguments, we may summarize some of the suggestions and findings of those modern scholars who are known as "form critics." Substantial similarities between Peter's and Paul's writing can be accounted for by their dependence upon a common tradition. Form critics remind us that a common tradition was not only incorporated into the Gospels but was also used for the New Testament epistles. The theory that the author of 1 Peter depended upon the Apostle Paul and his epistles "must now be rejected in favor of a common Petrine and Pauline use of a broadly varied (liturgical, parentic, and catechetical) tradition" and whoever the author of 1 Peter might be, this epistle "is the product of a Petrine tradition transmitted by Petrine tradents of a Petrine circle."[1] Another modern scholar has noted that there is no sign of direct dependence on Paul's letters in this epistle; the vocabulary of 1 Peter is quite different from Paul's,[2] and some common phrases may as well have come from Silvanus (5:12). This prominent member of the Christian Church in Jerusalem is usually identified with Silas of Acts 15:27ff, whose Roman name was Silvanus. From 2 Cor. 1:19 and from the salutations of 1 and 2 Thessalonians, we know that Silvanus was closely connected with Paul. He may have been one of those Jews who were at home in Greek, who joined Peter's mission, was with him in Rome, and, on the evidence of the epistle itself, is responsible for the good quality of the Greek used in 1 Peter.

The letter is rooted in older traditions, some of which go back to Jesus Himself. The author remembered the words of Jesus and applied them to a new situation. Thus, for instance, Matt. 5:10ff is echoed in 1 Peter 3:9, 14; and Matt. 5:16 in 1 Peter 2:12. E. G. Selwyn has observed that the words of the Sermon on the Mount as they are found in this epistle have "all the simplicity of direct testimony."[3] Who really wrote down the epistle, whether it was Peter "through the secretarial mediation of Silvanus" or somebody else soon after the death of the Apostle, somebody who belonged to a Petrine circle and who with others faithfully preserved the traditions connected with Peter, is not of primary importance. Whoever its author might be, the epistle is one of the precious documents of the first century that convey to us the spirit and

[1]John H. Elliott, "The Rehabilitation of an Exegetical Stepchild: I Peter in Recent Research," *Journal of Biblical Literature* 95:2 (1976) 247-8.

[2]Stephen Neill, *Jesus through Many Eyes: Introduction to the Theology of the New Testament* (Philadelphia: Fortress Press, 1976) 89.

[3]E. G. Selwyn, *The First Epistle of St. Peter* (London, 1958) 95.

the theological and ethical teachings of primitive Christianity.

Closely connected with the question of authorship is that of the nature of the epistle and its unity. There are those who cannot accept 1 Peter as a piece of genuine correspondence. Some regard it as a Roman baptismal liturgy given in two parts: the first, 1:3-4:11, for those who were being baptized, and the second, 4:12-5:11, addressed to the congregation as a whole. To others, 1 Peter represents the structure of the Easter Vigil service, when baptism was performed in the early Church. Suggestions such as these, attractive as they may be, have been subjected to penetrating criticism. The theme of baptism is surely present in the epistle, yet numerous references to baptism do not necessarily lead to the conclusion that this early Christian writing consists of a baptismal liturgy. This view about the nature of 1 Peter assumes that a very elaborate baptismal service existed at such an early date in a fixed form. Other critics, while rejecting the theory that 1 Peter was a baptismal liturgy, accepted this letter as being composed in two parts. The first, 1:3-4:11, was sent to churches that were not actually persecuted, according to their view, whereas the second, 4:12-5:14, was addressed to those churches that were suffering from persecution. All these theories divide the epistle and question its unity.

It is crucial for the unity of 1 Peter to know whether the persecution is presented as potential in the first part and actual in the second, whether or not Asian Christians were persecuted in the time of Peter or soon after his death. We do not know about an official persecution of Christians in Asia Minor before Domitian (A.D. 96). What kind of persecution, then, is referred to in 1 Peter? Was the imperial government involved? If it was, then it would be difficult to understand the exhortation of the author in 2:13-17: "Honor the emperor." We must suppose that the epistle does not point to the imperial government as the source and initiator of the persecution, but to the hostility and suffering inflicted by pagan neighbors, who represented the majority. They were hostile to the new religious group and disliked their way of life. In the past these newly baptized Christians had lived like gentiles, but now they did so no longer (4:3-4). This was irritating for the pagan majority. Their antagonism to- wards Christians, moreover, was probably encouraged by the local authorities. This was not official persecution but un- official harassment. In a recent commentary, J. N. D. Kelly argues strongly and convincingly that the letter is a unit and rejects the assumption on the basis of the text itself that the author addressed first Christians who were not being per- secuted and then those actually persecuted.[4] Peter speaks also in the first part about their martyrdom as a reality (1:6-7), and the kind of suffering spoken of here does not differ from that referred to in the second part (4:12ff). In both parts the author had the same churches in mind, and the theme of suffering, among various other themes, gives unity to this epistle.

The letter is addressed to Christians in five specified regions of Asia Minor. This is a circular letter, and the order of the Roman provinces given in its introduction, from Pontus to Bithynia, was the route that the bearer of the letter would be expected to take. The Christians in these regions are char- acterized "as aliens and exiles," as those without citizenship or permanent home in this world (1:1, 17). They are "the exiles of the dispersion," that is, of the *diaspora*. Originally the term *diaspora* referred to those Jews who lived outside Palestine. Here the term is not applied to them but to Chris- tians scattered throughout the world. Like "exiles," they hope one day to return to their homeland. Yet their minds are not set on an earthly Jerusalem, but on a heavenly one. Their "commonwealth is in heaven, and from it [they] await a Savior, the Lord Jesus Christ" (Phil. 3:20).

In the discussion that follows, therefore, we shall assume 1 Peter to be a genuine letter addressed to Christians in Asia Minor at the time of their persecution, which was limited to their part of the world. It is an epistle of courage in the face of trials and suffering. The letter is a unit in itself and not a composite of two letters. It is a real letter that manifests to us the spirit of primitive Christianity.

[4]J. N. D. Kelly, *A Commentary on the Epistles of Peter and of Jude* (New York: Harper and Row, 1969).

The Predominant Theme: Election

The unity of the epistle is reflected in its major themes, which convey a unified message. These are the themes of suffering, hope, salvation, and baptism, but most predominant is the theme of *election*. All the Christians who are scattered over the earth belong to the community of the elect. The Church knows that she is the elect of Israel. Christ is the living stone, rejected by man but chosen by God (2:4). He creates and upholds the people of God. These are the reasons why we should start with this theme, in order to bring out the central theological message of the letter, which is Christological.

The Christians to whom Peter addressed this letter are newly "chosen and destined by God the Father." At the very beginning he states the full meaning of their election (1:2). The source and initiative of their election are not in themselves but in "God the Father." They are not chosen because of their merits. Here the author is stressing the transcendent basis for their election, not that it was predestined. Election is enacted by baptism, "sanctified by the Spirit, for obedience to Jesus Christ and for sprinkling with his blood." As in Ex. 24:6-8, a text that describes the ratification of the old covenant, we have "obedience" and "sprinkling with blood" linked together here. The new covenant came into existence with the blood of Christ. All who have been baptized were baptized into Christ's death (Rom. 6:3), and thus brought into a new relationship with God. Election in 1 Peter is expressed in terms of an ancient Trinitarian formula: God the Father, the Spirit, and Jesus Christ. The recipient's baptism is also implied in it. What is revealed to them in their baptism is that they are chosen. The newly baptized are sanctified by the Spirit. They pledge their obedience to Christ, and they are now members of the new covenant and live with Him (Rom. 6:8).

Christians are asked to come to Christ, but this coming also involves belonging to the Church (2:4-10). Christ is the "living stone, rejected by men," but God through his "chosen" one accomplished His purposes. Calling Christ the "living stone" stresses that Jesus of Nazareth is the Risen Lord. Christians, on the other hand, bearing a likeness to Christ, are "living stones." They "have been born anew to a living hope" through the resurrection of Christ (1:3). The "living hope," like the "living stones," finds its source in the "living stone," that is, in the resurrected Christ. Christian hope rests on the divine act of salvation accomplished in Christ. This act is eschatological, and hope itself is an eschatological blessing of fulfillment.[5] Hope not merely helps Christians to endure suffering, but enables them to look beyond trials and persecutions (1:4). The Christian rejoices in his sufferings for he rejoices in his hope.

Christians are "living stones," that is, living persons who are incorporated into a "spiritual house" which is the temple of God, the Church, although the term "church" is not actually used in this epistle. By baptism they became living stones and acquired the role of a "holy priesthood to offer spiritual sacrifices." Christians are to offer themselves, in the words of St. Paul, "as a living sacrifice holy and acceptable to God" (Rom. 12:1), in "obedience to Jesus Christ" (1 Pet. 1:2) or "obedience to the truth" (1:22). After quoting three Old Testament texts in 2:6-8, where there is an image of stone which again points to Christ as the stone chosen by God (Is. 28:16; Ps. 118:22; Is. 8:14f), the author starts with a description of the new eschatological community. The names peculiar to the old Israel are now given to the New Israel, to the Christian Church: "But you are a chosen race, a royal priesthood, a holy nation, God's own people, that you may declare the wonderful deeds of him who called you out of darkness into his marvelous light" (2:9). These titles are taken from Ex. 19:5f, the most important passage for the election of Israel. The Christian community is "a chosen race," a priestly community. This text, however, does not refer to priests who perform their ministry *in* the Church at

[5]On ἐλπίς, see Gerhard Kittel, ed., *Theological Dictionary of the New Testament* 2 (Grand Rapids, Mich.: Eerdmans, 1964) 517-33. Hope in the Bible is not a consoling dream of the imagination that causes us to forget our present troubles, but is something rooted in a trust in God. Hope consists of confidence in God's protection and help. God is the hope of the righteous. Anything else, including the Temple, is false security.

the eucharistic gathering, but deals with and expresses the nature of the covenantal community,[6] which is rooted in Christ, and its witness *to* the world. The Church is a "holy nation," and the call to and demand for holiness is the same, for the people as well as for the priests. The author of 1 Peter 2:4-10 is not concerned with priestly or cultic acts, but is issuing an invitation to a way of life of holiness.[7] It should be recognized that Christians as a whole belong to a royal priesthood, which does not exclude the eucharistic priesthood, a priesthood that is called for a special ministry. This again should be understood against the background of the history and practices of ancient Israel, which was a kingdom of priests which did not exclude the Levitical priesthood. Peter in the quoted text stresses the election of the Church, which inherited Israel's vocation to be the light *to* the nations.

Through the sacrament of baptism men and women become a "chosen" people, a "royal priesthood," that is, dedicated to God's service to the pagan world (2:12), a "holy nation," set apart for God's special purposes. They were "no people" (οὐ λαός), now they are "God's own people" (λαὸς Θεοῦ), whose responsibility comes to be the proclamation of the saving acts of Him who brought them out of "darkness" into "light." Hence, in baptism they entered the Church and left paganism (2:10). The practical consequences of election are clearly spelled out in the verses that follow: the Christian's conduct in the pagan world, toward human institutions, especially toward slaves (2:11ff). All these areas of daily life, which we will discuss in the third part of this paper, the author includes as the ethical consequences or implications of the theological teaching or interpretation of the work of Christ and His Church.

---

[6]The same idea is expressed in Rev. 1:6; 5:10; and 20:6. Also in these verses, it is the community of the new covenant and not the role or status of some of its members that the author wanted to convey.

[7]See the excellent study of J. H. Elliott, "The Elect and the Holy," *Novum Testamentum*, supp. 12 (Leiden: E. J. Brill, 1966).

The Christology of the Suffering Servant

Christ, according to this epistle, "died for sins once for all" (3:18). This phrase "once for all" (ἅπαξ) indicates that Christ's sacrifice is unique and final, absolutely sufficient for the new relationship between God and men. He suffered and died "that he might bring us to God" (3:18). He was put "to death in the flesh," but was "made alive in the spirit," that is, raised from the dead (see 1 Tim. 3:16).

Christ's death, which brought redemption to man, was not the result of a sudden turn of historic events, but belonged to God's plan "before the foundation of the world," and now God's eternal purpose "was made manifest" with the incarnation of Christ (1:20). Peter, like Paul, incorporated into his writing some early Christian hymns which express what some call "high Christology." Paul uses hymns in this way in Phil. 2:5ff; Col. 1:15ff; and 1 Tim. 3:6. We may also have a hymn of the primitive Church in the passage under discussion, 1 Peter 1:20-21. The second verse of this hymn runs as follows: "Through him you have confidence in God, who raised him from the dead and gave him glory, so that your faith and hope are in God" (1:21). This hymn contains the fundamentals of New Testament theology: the preexistence of Christ, the incarnation, the death and resurrection of Christ, and finally His ascension.

Another ancient Christian liturgical hymn is quite probably contained in 1 Peter 2:21-25. Its major theme is Christ's suffering. He "bore our sins in his body on the tree," that is, He carried them up to the cross and accepted and endured punishment for them. By "his wounds" we "have been healed." The whole hymn is modeled upon the fourth song of the Suffering Servant of the Lord (Is. 53:5, 6, 12). Also, the theme of access to God through Christ, as it is formulated in 1 Peter 3:18, points to Is. 53:4. If we add these hymns from 1 Peter to the hymns and confessional passages of the Pauline tradition and compare them, we may conclude that the Suffering Servant Christology comes from the earliest stratum of Christian theology, which finally finds its origin in Jesus, who interpreted to His disciples His messianic role as the fulfillment of Is. 53.

One of the most difficult passages in 1 Peter is 3:18-21:

For Christ also died for sins once for all, the righteous for the unrighteous, that he might bring us to God, being put to death in the flesh but made alive in the spirit; in which he went and preached to the spirits in prison, who formerly did not obey, when God's patience waited in the days of Noah, during the building of the ark, in which a few, that is, eight persons, were saved through water. Baptism, which corresponds to this, now saves you, not as a removal of dirt from the body but as an appeal to God for a clear conscience, through the resurrection of Jesus Christ...

"In which" may be understood as referring to "the spirit." If it is understood in a temporal sense, then Christ's preaching took place in the interval between Good Friday and Easter morning. But who are these spirits in prison and what is preached to them? The exegetes are sharply divided on these questions. To some they are imprisoned angelic spirits (1 Enoch) who await their judgment and to whom Christ ascending to the Father proclaimed His supremacy. Some others, in view of 3:20 and 4:6, consider that probably the reference in 3:19 is to the souls of those who perished in the flood. And if Christ preached to all the dead (4:6) then he preached both to the angelic spirits (Gen. 6) and to those of Noah's generation.

Christ died for all, was raised for all, and proclaimed the good news to all. "The gospel was preached even to the dead" (4:6). With His descent into Hades Christ preached to all, including the righteous dead. The whole passage, 3:18-4:6, deals with the eschatological work of Christ in saving all who repent and believe in His word. "All" includes the saints of the old covenant. This is probably what the author had in mind. The tradition of Christ's descent is also reflected in Acts 2:27, 31; Rom. 10:6-8; and Eph. 4:8-10.

Of Noah's disobedient contemporaries, only Noah, his wife, and his three sons and their wives (Gen. 7:3) "were saved through water" (3:20). Peter now makes a comparison between baptism and water, between the saved of Noah's time and the recipients of the letter. Baptism, foreshadowed by the "water" of the flood, saves "now." Here we find a typological interpretation of Christian baptism. Water is the type and baptism is the antitype. Baptism does not save by the mere act of washing but "as an appeal to God for a clear conscience, through the resurrection of Jesus Christ," whose victory, indicated in 3:18, is now described as complete with His ascension to the Father. Without the power of the risen and ascended Christ, there is no Christian baptism. The uncertain meaning of the Greek word ἐπερώτημα (3:21), which is translated here as "appeal," makes the whole phrase difficult to understand. The evidence from the papyri indicates that ἐπερώτημα was used in contracts to mean "agreement" or "pledge." In the early Church, baptism was viewed as a seal of contract. Therefore, the phrase "a pledge to God for a clear conscience" suggests renunciation of "human passions" and of the gentile way of life (4:3), and a promise to live a life of obedience to Christ (1:2) and of doing "right" (3:17).

In chapter 4 the author again gives us the example of Christ's suffering of 3:18, as if he wanted to make his readers sure of its implications for Christians. Whoever imitates Christ in his suffering "has ceased from sin" (4:1)—not that he is sinless, but he will not be a compulsive, habitual sinner, for sin will not have dominion over him. He is not a slave of sin, for his life is directed by "the will of God" and no longer "by human passions" (4:2). What follows in 4:3-6 illustrates and enforces what was already written in 4:1-2. The gentiles "abuse" Christians who have given up their former pagan way of life and refuse to join again "in the same wild profligacy," and for this they will be responsible to Christ, "who is ready to judge the living and the dead," that is, all the people (4:3-5). This judgment is just, for the dead heard the gospel and were given an opportunity for salvation (4:6; 1:6), that "they might live in the spirit like God."

Christ is "ready to judge," and the author adds that the end is "at hand" (4:7). This eschatological perspective colors the ethical teachings of the epistle. Because the end is around the corner Asian Christians are exhorted to use their baptismal gifts and to manifest "love for one another" (4:8). The waiting for the end intensifies their tension with the world and inspires them on the road to a life of holiness. In the perspective of the epistle, the persecution of the Asian Christians appears as a sign that points to the end. Christ is the Lord (3:15), and His coming is to be expected (1:7, 13; 4:13; 5:1). This hope of an imminent end gives to the ethical teaching a special importance, as it does in St. Paul's letters to the Thessalonians.

The Call to Light

The reminder of what God has done for the salvation of men is followed by a call to Christians to live in the light of what has been revealed to them. This new way of life is different from what they practiced while they were pagans (1:14; 2:11; 4:2f). The words "passions" and "ignorance" point to a gentile background of these people, who were recent converts to Christianity. They must now be prepared for the final revelation of Christ, His second coming, and center their hopes on God, who is holy; and the people that belong to Him should be holy in everything that they undertake. They are God's special people, set apart for His service, and they are asked to practice a life of moral purity. They are called to live "in fear," or reverently, or in the awe that a man experiences when he finds himself in the presence of God. While living in the world, these Christians are to exercise "good conduct among the gentiles," in order to bring the gentiles to God by their "good deeds" (2:20; 3:17; 4:13). Gentiles might be moved by their good example and may glorify God on the day of their conversion, when they will receive mercy and be baptized (2:12, 10).

The recipients of this letter are already baptized, cleansed, and able to "love one another earnestly from the heart"

(2:17; 3:8; 4:8). Baptism is a rebirth by the "word of God," the gospel. These newly born are exhorted to long for "the pure spiritual milk." In rabbinical literature "milk" stands for the Law, and in this epistle for the gospel. This food will make them "grow up to salvation." They already "have tasted the kindness of the Lord" (2:3). This is a quotation from Psalm 34:8, which was used in the early Church during the eucharistic service.

As in 1 John, the evidence, the sign of holiness, is above all love of the brethren. Christians are called to share with one another the gifts that they received and to use them for their own growth as well as for that of the community to which they belong. They are particularly exhorted to show "love for one another, since love covers a multitude of sins" (4:8; Pr. 10:12). If love is practiced, probably sins will be forgiven. "Having purified your souls by your obedience to the truth for a sincere love of the brethren, love one another earnestly from the heart" (1:22). This is love that is rooted in baptism and obedience to the gospel. In conformity with Matt. 5:43-48, the author of this epistle calls all to the new way of life and holiness: "Do not return evil for evil or reviling for reviling; but on the contrary bless, for to this you have been called, that you may obtain a blessing" (3:9). This is a call to "overcome evil with good" (Rom. 12:21).

Their spirituality can be seen in maintaining "good conduct" among the gentiles and in their love for one another. This is one line which separates these Christians from those who belong to the world. There is, however, another line of separation between them that is "marked by the tears and sometimes the blood of the persecuted" Christians.[8] And we should never forget that this epistle is addressed to the persecuted Christian communities. Concerned with their plight, the author of this epistle encouraged them to endure their ordeals. He points to the suffering of Christ. Just as He suffered and suffered unjustly, so will His disciples. "Since therefore Christ suffered in the flesh, arm yourselves with the same thought" (4:1). Christ gave them an example, that

[8]Selwyn, p. 82.

they "should follow in his steps" (2:21). In the New Testament there is another passage in addition to the one found in 1 Peter which belongs to "example Christology,"[9] where Jesus washed the feet of His Apostles as an example to them (John 13:15f). Both are addressed to and preserved in the Christian communities at the time of persecution. The "example Christology" of Peter and John is consistent with Paul's view that we are children of God and fellow heirs with Christ, "provided we suffer with him in order that we may also be glorified with him" (Rom. 8:17).

If one suffers as a Christian "let him glorify God," let him "rejoice" insofar as he shares Christ's sufferings (4:13ff), the author tells the persecuted Christian bodies. This phenomenon of joy in suffering appears as an essential characteristic of New Testament experience. The Apostles, in the Book of Acts, rejoiced "that they were counted worthy to suffer dishonor for his name" (5:41).

This all-pervading theme of Christian rejoicing in Christ's suffering is rooted in the believer's incorporation into Christ in baptism. That the "suffering" has as its ultimate reference the death of Christians in baptism appears as an understanding common to St. Paul and primitive Christianity.[10] "Do you not know that all of us who have been baptized into Christ Jesus were baptized into his death? . . . For if we have been united with him in a death like his, we shall certainly be united with him in a resurrection like his" (Rom. 6:3-5). There is nothing morbid about this Christian view of suffering because it is undergone in unity with Christ Himself. The recipients of the letter have already been baptized and introduced into the Kingdom of God. Through baptism they are set on the road to inherit the "promised land." They did not have Peter's privilege of seeing Christ, yet they love Him, believe in Him (1:8), and are full of joy. Their faith and love and the living hope to which they "have been born anew" and whose source is in the resurrection of Christ (1:3) will lead them to the "salvation" of their "souls" (1:9). The

[9]See Herold Weis, "Foot Washing in the Johannine Community," *Novum Testamentum* 21:4 (1979) 298ff.
[10]See the article on πάσχω in Kittel 5:904ff.

term "soul" stands here for the whole man (see 1:22; 2:11, 25; 3:20; 4:19).

"The fiery ordeal" through which these Asian Christians were passing is a sign that the judgment of God has already started, and that it has begun with "the household of God," with the Church (4:17). What then, the author wonders, "will be the end of those who do not obey the gospel of God?" Those who are "reproached for the name of Christ," which means as Christians or because of Christ, are "blessed," and "the spirit of glory and of God rests upon" them (4:14). God's Holy Spirit, the source of glory, who is present and rests upon the persecuted Christians of Asia Minor, anticipates the future glory to come. None is to suffer as a "wrongdoer" (κακοποιός) or as a "mischief-maker" (ἀλλοτριεπίσκοπος, 4:15). This last phrase is translated as "one who interferes in other people's affairs," or even as "revolutionary" (Moffat). To share in Christ's suffering implies suffering without resorting to violence, and "this is the very principle of the incarnation."[11]

Human Institutions in the Divine Order

This leads us to the attitude of 1 Peter toward the pagan state: what should Christian conduct be toward human institutions? As people in a foreign country, whose stay in this world is short, Christians are asked to show respect for the civil authorities. In this passage, 2:12-17, the author expresses the common body of teaching of the ancient Church before the Domitian persecution (c. A.D. 96). Human institutions have a definite place in the divine order and exist for the good of society. The very term κτίσις, used in 1 Peter 2:13, may indicate that this human institution belongs to God's order of creation,[12] without being divine. As "servants of God" Christians are free, and as free men they "render

[11]C. F. D. Moule, *The Birth of the New Testament* (London: Adam & Charles Black, 1962) 139.

[12]See the commentary on 1 Peter in the *Jerome Biblical Commentary* (Englewood Cliffs, N. J.: Prentice Hall, 1968) 365.

unto Caesar" what belongs to Caesar. They respect and honor all men, yet they are asked to fear God only (see 1:17), and to honor the emperor. At the time of the writing of this epistle, the cult of the emperor had not yet been introduced. What is given in 1 Peter is not different from the approach of St. Paul in Rom. 13.

These two passages, Rom. 13:1-7 and 1 Peter 2:13-17, express the common tradition, the common body of the teaching of the ancient Church, regarding the governing authorities. The common material and common approach that is found in these two epistles could be satisfactorily explained in that Peter and Paul both drew upon a common source. At the same time, we must also notice the differences between them. In Rom. 13 the material is more developed than in 1 Peter 2. This may point to the more primitive character of the tradition incorporated by Peter. Both Romans and 1 Peter were written before the rise of the emperor cult, and their treatments of the church-empire problem are both given in an eschatological context. "The day is at hand" (Rom. 13:12) and the "end of all things is at hand" (1 Pet. 4:7). The basic assumption is that the state is pagan, the government reasonable, and the time is "at hand." Both authors stress love in brotherly and social relations, against the background of the intense expectation of the last things. While Christians live in the "overlapping of ages," their attitude toward the empire is rather positive. They are asked to be subject to authority "not only to avoid God's wrath but also for the sake of conscience" (Rom. 13:5). Peter wrote to Christians in Asia Minor who were persecuted and, as we have mentioned, were accused, among other things, of being ἀλλοτριεπίσκοποι (4:15). On the other hand, Paul wrote to the Church in Rome, which was not persecuted at the time Romans was written. It is quite possible, however, that some Jewish Christians, expelled from Rome by Claudius around A.D. 48 and allowed to return by Nero in A.D. 54, were tempted to take the Zealot's attitude toward the Roman authorities. It has been suggested that Paul had this in mind and repudiated the revolutionary tendencies of the Zealot movement in Rom. 13:2: "He who resists the authorities resists what God appointed, and those who resist will incur judgment."[13] Neither Paul nor Peter deal with the possibility that the benevolent government may one day be transformed into a tyrannical rule, under the domination of demonic powers. By earthly authority they mean only one that administers justice for the good of mankind. If they had been confronted with a Domitian, they would have resisted his claims. Absolute loyalty to God and His divine order would have led them to resist any type of government that tried to overstep the bounds allotted to it.

Although both epistles reject revolutionary activity, their teaching of obedience to the qualified, limited authority of human institutions contains a revolutionary element. The possibility of resistance is implied, although violence is excluded. The author of 1 Peter also, for instance, makes radical claims for Jesus. He writes to the Christians to honor the emperor, but this same emperor stands under the judgment of God revealed in Jesus Christ (1:17). Christians are called to suffer in the name of Christ. This call to suffering implies resistance. Many have suffered without being Christians. But Christians are called to suffer in the name of Christ, that is, to bear witness to His suffering on the cross which marks the victory over death itself. This is what is new in the suffering of the Asian Christians to whom 1 Peter is addressed. Not any kind of suffering, "let none of you suffer as a murderer, or as a thief, or a wrongdoer, or a mischief-maker" (4:15), but only suffering in which they share Christ's suffering is blessed, is Christian suffering.

Following the passage that deals with the Christian attitude toward human institutions are the so-called *Haustafelen*, short exhortations related to the conduct of slaves and masters. We find them in Paul's letters also (Eph. 6:9; Col. 4:1). What is of immediate interest to us is the fact that Peter develops the theme of suffering in connection with admonitions to servants in Christian households (2:21-25). If they suffer for doing what is wrong, it is not to their credit. But if they suffer unjustly, then they should remember Christ's example and "follow in his steps." These slaves are no longer

[13]C. H. Dodd, *The Epistle of Paul to the Romans* (New York, 1932) 203.

what they were before. "Like sheep" they were wandering from one place to another, but "now" Christ is their "shepherd" (ποιμὴν) who cares for His flock, and He also is their "guardian" (ἐπίσκοπος).[14] Peter, like Paul, in Philemon, shows an attitude toward slaves that was novel for the time. Slaves are addressed with love as brethren, as equals in Christ. This attitude changed the relationship between slaves and masters and in the course of subsequent history and greater Christian influence finally undermined the system of slavery in the Roman empire.

Here the theological basis and inspiration of the Christian approach to governing institutions and to slavery is revealed. Christ suffered and died to save human beings, not the state. They are created in the image and likeness of God; human institutions are not. Jesus taught, and the Church has been praying: "Thy kingdom come." With this petition Christians daily underline where and to whom their ultimate loyalty belongs, and with this petition they reduce all human institutions and human ideology to their proper and rightful place in God's plan of salvation. There is no utopianism in 1 Peter or in any other book of the New Testament, "for the form of this world is passing away" (1 Cor. 7:31). Jesus did not ask for the Church's withdrawal from the world, but prayed that God keep her from the evil one (John 17:15), that is, from attacks of evil powers, from the temptation to identify herself with the world, as well as from isolation from the world and its problems.

There is no system of social ethics developed in the New Testament. But there is much in it about the gospel's impact upon social relationships and the gospel's demand for social responsibility. Neither Jesus nor the early Church considered themselves called to create programs for a perfect society. The Church is not tied to any particular structure of society, and yet she is called to perform a mission and service in and for the world.

The passages we discussed (1 Pet. 2:13ff and 4:12ff) have been characterized as "conservative," as defending the

---

[14]It is worth noting that whereas ἐπίσκοπος came into use as a title in the Christian ministry, ποιμὴν never became a technical term.

status quo. We have rejected this contention and interpretation by pointing to their radical implication, to the tension between the demands of and claims for Christ and the world. The meaning of these texts transcends the particular historically conditioned situation in which they were written. Yet their authority and application to our modern problems and social demands is not external or objective, but an authority that can be realized only within the life of the community, within the ongoing history of the Church. The New Testament is complete, but the history of the Church that came into existence after the death and resurrection of Christ has continued, and from it we can derive some principles that are of permanent importance for the Church of any age. One is that the Church should never try to use violence to fight evil, for violence produces violence without bringing evil to an end, and instead creates new conditions for its growth and spread. The Church must and should resist evil in any form without resorting to violence. By saying "Do not return evil for evil" (3:9), Peter echoes the words of Christ (Luke 6:27-28; see also Rom. 12:17). "But the face of the Lord is against those that do evil" (1 Pet. 3:12).

In 1 Peter we find Christological and ethical teachings closely interwoven. Both are given in the context of the Christian life under the constant threat of ill-treatment by pagan neighbors. Christianity for the author is a way of life, dying to sin and living to righteousness (2:24).[15] And this new life finds its strength in a new relation with God that has been brought about in baptism. The person of Christ is presented in this epistle as one who is alive, present, the example as well as the power given to those who pass through persecution and suffering. He is the shepherd, and not simply a historical figure of the past.

Conclusion

This epistle is one of the first examples of primitive eschatology in the New Testament. The end has already be-

[15]W. C. Van Unnik, "Christianity according to I Peter," *Expository Times* 68 (1956-1957) 79-83.

gun and the persecuted Church bears witness to it. Christ, His death and resurrection, is the beginning of the end. And, finally, to the question: "If all the rest of the New Testament had been lost and we had only this single specimen of early Christian writing, would we lack anything that is essential to Christian belief and to the life of godliness?"[16] we can answer that all essential elements of Christian theological and ethical teaching are presented concretely, uncompromisingly, and with inspiring faith in the "Guardian of [our] souls" (2:25). The author of this epistle uses both doctrinal and liturgical material spontaneously, without artificially introducing it into his composition; he does not present it in blocks that would be easily distinguishable. Moral exhortations together with liturgical references and doctrinal teachings are interwoven into one unit, which is our present letter.

Toward the end of the letter, the author makes a final reference to persecution. It is personified as the devil "seeking someone to devour" (5:8). He always tries to use suffering for his own purposes and to remove those who suffer from the path of faith. Be "firm" in your faith, writes Peter. In resisting the devil, believers should also know that persecution and suffering are part of Christian existence "throughout the world" (5:9), for they have been part of Christ's life and ministry. His temptations and suffering have been experienced in the life of His followers. But Christians, according to 1 Peter, should know that they are not left alone in their ordeal, not left to their own resources, for He "who has called [them] to his eternal glory in Christ" (1:2; 2:9) will Himself "strengthen" them (5:10).

What the Christians of the first century believed and professed about God, Christ, the Church, salvation, and what the life of holiness consists of is expressed or reflected in this epistle.

[16]Neill, p. 92.

CHAPTER 9

THE SYMBOL OF
THEANDRIC SYNTHESIS

*We in the Church stand before
the awesome symbol of the Lifegiving Cross. In this Cross earth is met
by heaven, man is met by God, despair is met by hope, death is met by
life. For the Church, then, the Cross
is the consummation of human history, in which we know that a new
creation was born in the midst of our
world.*

Metropolitan Philip

Thomas Hopko, who teaches dogmatic theology at St. Vladimir's Seminary, has become one of the leading young Orthodox theologians in the new world. His vision of what the Orthodox Church is and must be has by now been made only too clear in his many written and oral presentations. In this chapter, Fr. Hopko again establishes this vision, but now as it is seen in the tree of the cross. As the symbol of the God-man synthesis, the cross is first presented by the author in its historical and liturgical contexts. Then, using Scripture and the Fathers of the Church, he brings the reader to the vision that it is only the cross which "gathers in itself the entire mystery of salvation . . . embraces in itself the entire mystery of the spiritual life." Thus, we are shown the tree of the cross as the symbol of the theandric synthesis.

J. J. A.

The Tree of the Cross

by

THOMAS HOPKO

> ". . . the tree of the Cross is raised in the
> midst of the earth . . . and the whole
> world is filled with boundless joy."

On September 14 the Christian churches of East and West
celebrate the festival of the Exaltation of the Holy Cross. The
liturgical celebration of the feast originated in Jerusalem in
the fourth century as the commemoration of the dedication of
the Church of the Resurrection. It soon came to be associated
with the commemoration of the discovery of the cross of
Christ by Helen, the mother of Emperor Constantine the
Great, who traditionally came to power and gave freedom to
Christians because of his vision of the cross surrounded by
the words: "In this sign you will conquer!" When the cross
was seized by the Persians in the seventh century and recap-
tured, to be returned by the Emperor Heraclius, the feast of
the Exaltation of the Cross was introduced in the capital city
of Constantinople. From there it spread throughout the empire, being introduced in Rome at the end of the same seventh
century by Pope Sergius.[1]

[1]See Leonid Ouspensky and Vladimir Lossky, *The Meaning of Icons*
(Boston, 1969) 151-3. For the more legendary accounts of the origin of
the festival see K. Nikol'skii, *Posobie k izucheniiu Ustava Bogosluzheniia
Pravoslavnoi Tserkvi* (St. Petersburg, 1900) 532-6; and Jacobus de Voragine,
The Golden Legend (New York, 1969) 543-50. See also *Liturgy: The Holy
Cross*, vol. 1, no. 1 of the *Liturgy* series put out by the Liturgical Con-

In the Eastern Orthodox Church today the feast is officially called the Universal Exaltation of the Precious and Lifegiving Cross. It is one of the twelve major festivals of the church year, celebrated with particular solemnity. On the feast itself, which is observed as a fasting day regardless of the day of the week on which it falls, the celebration of the Eucharist is preceded by a solemn Vigil during which the cross, decorated with flowers, is brought in procession with candles and incense into the middle of the church. There the bishop or priest elevates it in the four directions of the universe with cruciform benedictions, accompanied by the chanting of *Kyrie eleison* as many as seventy or a hundred times for each petition of the Litany of Fervent Supplication.[2]

The Exaltation of the Holy Cross was celebrated in the Byzantine empire, and in later Orthodox nation-states, as a kind of "political holy day." The elevation of the cross in the hands of the priest was the official exaltation of the unifying standard of political and social, as well as ecclesiastical and spiritual, life. The main hymn of the feast was sung as a kind of national anthem:

O Lord save Thy people and bless Thine inheritance.
Grant victories to the Orthodox Christians over their adversaries.
And by the virtue of the Cross, preserve Thy habitation.[3]

The veneration of the Holy Cross, with a special song of adoration, functioned as a pledge of allegiance:

Before Thy Cross we bow down in worship, O Master,
And Thy holy resurrection we glorify.[4]

ference in Washington, D. C. in 1980. The present essay was in substance first published in this issue.

[2]For the rubrics and complete text of the festival see Nikol'skii, and, in English, Mother Mary and Archimandrite Kallistos Ware, trs., *The Festal Menaion* (London, 1969) 131-63.

[3]The original text for the troparion entreats victories for the Orthodox king over the barbarians (*Festal Menaion*, p. 141).

[4]This hymn is sung with prostrations at each service, and replaces the Trisagion at the eucharistic service.

Everyone and everything was sealed with the sign of the cross. All actions were undertaken, at least theoretically, by the power of the cross, and for its glory and honor.

While the political, or as Vladimir Lossky calls them, the "Constantinian," elements of the liturgical offices of the Exaltation of the Cross remain, some of the texts have been altered and the prayers are now given a purely spiritual meaning.[5] The fact that man's life in its totality, and indeed the life of the entire world and the whole of creation, finds its source and fulfillment, its content and purpose in the cross of Christ is still proclaimed and celebrated in the festival, but this life is no longer identified with the well-being and destiny of the Christian empire, or one or another of the Orthodox nation-states.

Whatever the historical origins of the feast of the Exaltation of the Cross, and whatever its political significance and function in the past, the feast continues to preserve for God's people that for which it was inspired and instituted by the Holy Spirit in the Church, namely, to provide a liturgical celebration, contemplation, and adoration of Christ's Holy Cross as the unique symbol that truly unites in itself, in mystical fulness, all of the deepest truths about God and man, nature and history, being and life itself. Thus, the hymns of the feast:

Rejoice, O life-bearing Cross,
The invincible trophy of godliness,
The door of paradise,
The foundation of the faithful,
The protection guarding the Church,
  by which corruption is utterly destroyed
  and the power of death swallowed up
  and we are exalted to heaven from earth.
The invincible weapon,
The adversary of demons,
The glory of martyrs,
The true beauty of saints,

[5]Ouspensky and Lossky, pp. 151-2.

The haven of salvation
   which gives great mercy to the world.

Rejoice, O Cross of the Lord,
Through which humanity has been freed from the
   curse.
The true standard of joy.
In your exaltation, O Most Precious Cross,
   you scatter the enemies.
You are our helper.
The power of kings,
The strength of the righteous,
The divine beauty of priests,
   delivering from peril all who sign themselves with
   you.
The staff by which we the flock are tended,
The weapon of peace round which angels stand in
   awe,
Divine glory of Christ, which gives great mercy to the
   world.

Rejoice, O Guide to the blind,
The healer of the sick,
The resurrection of the dead.
O Precious Cross which raises us who have fallen
   into corruption,
By which the curse is destroyed and incorruption
   blossoms forth,
By which we earthborn creatures are deified and the
   devil utterly destroyed.
We behold you today exalted in the hands of the
   high priest.
We exalt Him who was lifted upon you.
And we venerate you from which we richly draw great
   mercy.[6]

_____
[6]Great Vespers hymns of the feast.

The Theandric Symbol

Some of the greatest Church Fathers taught that it was neither accidental nor arbitrary that the incarnate Word of God, Jesus Christ, redeemed His creation by means of the cross. They say, on the contrary, that it was necessary that the Deathless One should die *on the wood*. They see in the cross, both in its substance and form, the fullest possible revelation of God, which could be made in no other way. They comprehend in the cross the all-embracing, all-encompassing manifestation of the theandric mystery at the center of being and time, which could only be accomplished by means of the cruciform Tree. Thus, St. Athanasius writes in his incomparable essay *On the Incarnation of the Word of God:*

> But if any honest Christian wants to know why He suffered death on the Cross and not in some other way, we answer thus: in no other way was it expedient for us, indeed the Lord offered for our sakes the one death that was supremely good. He had come to bear the curse that lay on us; and how could He "become a curse" otherwise than by accepting the accursed death? And that death is the cross, for it is written: "Cursed is every one who hangs on a tree." [Gal. 3:13; Deut. 21:23] Again the death of the Lord is the ransom for all, and by it "the middle wall of partition" is broken down and the call of the Gentiles comes about. [Eph. 2:14] ... Again, we see the fitness of His death and of those outstretched arms: it was that He might draw His ancient people with the one arm and the Gentiles with the other, and to join both peoples together in Himself. Even so, He foretold the manner of His redeeming death: "I, if I be lifted up, will draw all men to Myself." [John 12:32] Again, the air is the sphere of the devil, the enemy of our race, who, having fallen from heaven endeavors with the other evil spirits ... to keep souls from the truth and to hinder the progress of those who are trying to

follow it. . . . But the Lord came to overthrow the devil and to purify the air and to make a way for us up to heaven . . . This had to be done through death, but by what other kind of death could it be done, except by a death in the air, that is, on the cross? . . . Fitting indeed then, and wholly consonant was the death on the cross for us; and we can see how reasonable it was, and why it is that the salvation of the world could be accomplished in no other way. Even on the cross He did not hide Himself from sight, rather, He made all creation witness to the presence of its Maker.[7]

And St. Gregory of Nyssa, in many ways the disciple of the great Athanasius, continues the reflection on what he calls the "traditional teaching":

And as to the Cross, whether it possesses some other deeper meaning, those who are skilled in mysticism may explain; but however that may be, the traditional teaching which has reached us is as follows:

Since all things in the Gospel, both words and deeds, have a sublime and heavenly meaning . . . in the *fact* of this death we must contemplate the human feature, while in the *manner* of it we must be desirous to find the divine. For since it is the property of the Godhead to pervade all things, and to extend itself through the length and breadth of the substance of existence in every part . . . this is the very thing we learn from the figure of the Cross. It is divided into four parts so that there are the projections, four in number, from the central point where the whole converges upon itself, because He who at the hour of His death was stretched upon it is He who binds together all things into Himself and by Himself brings to one harmonious agreement the diverse natures of actual beings.

Since then all creation looks to Him, and is about and

[7]Athanasius, *On the Incarnation*, tr. and ed. A Religious of C.S.M.V. (Crestwood, N. Y.: SVS Press, 1980) 54-5.

around Him, and through Him is coherent in itself ...
it is from sight that the mighty Paul starts when he
initiates the people of Ephesus in the mysteries and
imbues them through his instructions with the power
of knowing "with all the saints what is the breadth
and length and height and depth, and to know the love
of Christ which surpasses knowledge, that you may be
filled with all the fulness of God." (Eph. 3:18-19)

In fact he designates each projection of the Cross by
its proper name. The upper part he calls height, the
lower depth, and the side extensions breadth and
length. And in another passage he makes his thought
still clearer ... when he says "that at the name of
Jesus every knee should bow, of things in heaven, and
things in earth, and things under the earth; and that
every tongue should confess that Jesus Christ is Lord,
to the glory of God the Father." (Phil. 2:10-11) In
that passage he includes in one name the center and
projecting bars, calling "things on earth" all that is in
the middle between things in heaven and things under
the earth. Such is the lesson we learn in regard to the
mystery of the Cross.[8]

The liturgical texts of the Exaltation in the Orthodox
Church see the outstretched arms of the Savior prefigured in
the outstretched praying arms of Jacob, Moses, Joshua, Jonah,
and others of the old covenant righteous whose sufferings
are fulfilled and perfected in the sufferings of God's Son
upon the cross. The services also see in the crucified Word of
God, with His arms outstretched, the open book of life for
all to read and understand; literate and illiterate, wise and
simple, learned and lowly. For there is no moment, say the
saints, when the divine Word more powerfully and eloquently
proclaims the great mercy of God than when He hangs suspended in silence upon the tree of the cross. At this moment
the God who is love is ultimately revealed in all His divine
splendor and glory. At this moment the Son of His love

[8]Gregory of Nyssa, *The Great Catechism* 22.

glorifies Him and is glorified by Him with the divine glory which they share from before the foundation of the world. Thus Jesus Himself speaks, according to the Gospel of St. John:

> "The hour has come for the Son of Man to be glorified. Truly, truly I say to you, unless a grain of wheat falls into the earth and dies, it remains alone; but if it dies, it bears much fruit." (12:23-24)

> "Now my soul is troubled. And what shall I say? 'Father, save me from this hour'? No, for this purpose I have come to this hour. Father, glorify thy name." (12:27-28)

> "Now is the judgment of the world, now shall the ruler of this world [the devil] be cast out; and I, when I am lifted up from the earth, will draw all men to myself." He said this to show by what death he was to die. (12:31-33)

> "Now the Son of Man is glorified and in him God is glorified; if God is glorified in him, God will also glorify him in himself, and glorify him at once." (13:31-32)

> "Father, the hour has come; glorify Thy Son that the Son may glorify Thee." (17:1)

The cross is the glory of Christ. It is the glory of God and the glory of man. It is the meeting point of heaven and earth; the focal point of the theandric mystery of life; the end point of history; the starting point of the new creation of the Kingdom of God in the midst of the earth. Christ came for this hour; and, in the deepest sense, for this hour the world itself was made—for the moment when all is fulfilled and consummated in the Pascha of the Lamb of God, who was destined before the foundation of creation to be slain upon the cross for the life of the world.[9]

[9]See Georges Florovsky, *Creation and Redemption*, vol. 3 of his *Collected Works* (Belmont, Mass.: Nordland, 1976) 95-159.

Today the Cross is exalted and the world is sanctified.
For Thou who art enthroned with the Father and the
 Holy Spirit have spread out Thine arms upon it,
And have drawn the world to the knowledge of Thee,
 O Christ.
Make worthy of divine glory those who have put their
 trust in Thee.[10]

The Wood of the Tree

As the perfect symbol—the symbol most real and the reality most symbolic—the cross gathers into unity every element of God's gracious dispensation in creation and redemption for our celebration, contemplation, and praise. It does
so not only by its form, but also by its substance. It is the *tree*
of the cross, the lifegiving *wood* by which humanity is healed.
By a tree the first Adam was cast out of paradise; and by a
tree the last Adam brings him back. By his disobedience to
God the first Adam was cut off from the tree of life and given
over unto death. By His obedience to the Father "unto death,
even death on a cross," the last Adam restores humanity to
communion with the tree of life, which is itself the most
precious tree of the cross. The liturgy of the Exaltation cele-
brates this central mystery of man's being and life:

O thrice-blessed Tree on which Christ the King was
 stretched,
Through thee the beguiler [the devil] fell who tempted
 humanity with the tree.
He was caught in the trap set by God who was crucified
 upon thee in the flesh,
Granting peace to our souls.

The Wood made famous in song,
O Cross on which Christ was suspended,
The whirling sword that guarded Eden was fearful of
 thee.

[10]The Hymn of Light at the Matins of the feast.

And the dread cherubim gave way before Christ who
   was crucified upon thee,
Granting peace to our souls.

Let all the trees of the forest rejoice,
For their nature is sanctified by Christ who planted
   them in the beginning,
And who was Himself outstretched on the Tree.
At its exaltation today we worship Him and glorify
   thee.

O Mother of God, thou art a mystical paradise
Who brought forth Christ without seed.
He has planted on earth the lifegiving Tree of the
   Cross.
Therefore at its Exaltation today, we worship Him and
   glorify thee.

In paradise of old the wood stripped me bare . . .
But now the wood of the Cross that clothes man with
   the garment of life has been set up in the midst of
   the earth,
Behold, it is exalted, O People!
Let us with one mind raise our cry to God in faith:
Thy temple is full of thy glory![11]

There are three readings from the Old Testament at the
festival of the Exaltation of the Cross. The first tells how
Moses threw the tree into the bitter waters of Marah, and the
waters became sweet and satisfied the thirst of God's newly
liberated people.[12] The second reading, from Proverbs, shows
how the tree of the cross, which the epistle reading at the
festal Eucharist proclaims as the Wisdom of God, is prefigured in the Old Testamental Wisdom, which is "the tree
of life to them that lay hold upon her; and happy is everyone
who retains her." The third reading is from Isaiah. Here the

[11]Canon hymns from the Matins of the feast.
[12]The three Old Testament readings are Ex. 15:22-16:1; Pr. 3:11-18;
and Is. 60:11-16. The epistle reading at the Divine Liturgy is 1 Cor.
1:18-24.

old covenant conviction that the city of Jerusalem—especially the temple, and more especially the sanctuary—is the "footstool" of the Lord is contemplated in the light of the New Testament conviction that the Lord's final and perfect "footstool" is the most Holy Cross. The line from Psalm 99 is used throughout the liturgical celebration of the Exaltation in this way: "Exalt ye the Lord our God, and worship at His footstool, for He [it] is holy" (Ps. 99:5).

The Symbol of Victory and Light

At the Holy Eucharist of the feast, Psalm 99 is also used to introduce the epistle and the Gospel reading, which is the passion according to John. Psalms 22 and 74 are used for the antiphonal songs at the Eucharist. And the Gospel reading at the Vigil, which contains Jesus' words about drawing all people to Himself when He is lifted up from the earth, is introduced with lines from Psalm 98: "All the ends of the earth have seen the salvation (victory) of our God. Sing unto the Lord a new song, for He has done marvelous things."

At the festival of the Exaltation of the Holy Cross all the ends of the earth see the victory of God. They behold His glory and rejoice in His salvation. Although kept as a day of fasting, the festival is a day of liturgical rejoicing. The message of the cross is glory and joy. It is the apostolic message that "nothing can separate us from the love of God in Christ Jesus" since "we are more than conquerors through him who loved us." The victory is won. The Kingdom is given. Death has been destroyed and the demons are demolished. Darkness is filled with light. And life reigns in abundance by the death of Him who is Life itself, triumphant in His resurrection, which could never have been had He not first emptied Himself in the majestic humility of His eternal divinity, exalted upon the tree of the Cross.[13]

Let us be glad today and sing in honor of the feast.
With joyful face and lips let us cry aloud:

[13]See Florovsky; also N. Arseniev, *The Revelation of Life Eternal* (New York: SVS Press, n.d.) 61-100.

Thou has accepted the condemnation, O Christ.
Thou wast spit upon and scourged.
Thou wast wrapped in a purple robe.
Thou wast exalted upon the Cross.
The sun and the moon saw Thee and hid their light.
The earth quaked with fear.
The veil in the temple was torn in two.
Grant now Thy precious Cross to us
As our guardian and protector and defense against
   demons,
That embracing it we may cry aloud:
Save us, O Cross, by thy might.
Make us holy, O Cross by thy exaltation today.
For thou hast been to us as our Light,
And the salvation of our souls.[14]

The cross gathers in itself the entire mystery of salvation, and as such, embraces in itself the entire mystery of the spiritual life. To take up the cross and to live within its power is salvation. It is the Kingdom of God, defined by the Apostle as "the peace and the joy and the righteousness in the Holy Spirit." It is *theosis*, deification, the becoming God by grace that is the center and goal of human being and life.

A myth abounds today that the Eastern Orthodox Church is not the church of the cross, but the church of the transfiguration and resurrection. Some even claim that the "imitation of Christ," which is a scriptural, apostolic admonition, is a western peculiarity, unknown to the exalted and glorious mystical spirituality of the Greek Fathers and saints. But, as Fr. Florovsky reminds us, "salvation is completed on Golgotha, not on Tabor, and the Cross of Jesus was foretold even on Tabor."[15] (Cf. Luke 9:31) For the Tabor light which surrounds the risen Christ in His glorious victory over death, i.e., in His saving resurrection, is the light which enters the world by way of the cross, and no other way. The holy people of God who have attained to this light have come to it in this very way, and every one of them bears witness to

[14]The Lity hymn of Vespers.
[15]Florovsky, p. 99.

this truth. We could not find a more fitting witness than the most mystical and charismatic St. Symeon the New Theologian:

> Clothed in the radiant garments of the Spirit, we abide in God and He in us. Through grace we become gods and sons of God and are illumined by the light of His knowledge. . . .

> It is right that we should first of all bend our necks to the yoke of Christ's commandments . . . walking in them and zealously even unto death renewing ourselves forever and making of ourselves a fresh paradise of God until, through the Holy Spirit, the Son and the Father enter into us and dwell in us.

> Let us look then how to glorify God. The only way we can glorify Him is as the Son glorified Him. . . . But by that, by which the Son glorified His Father was the Son Himself glorified by the Father. Let us strive then to do what the Son has done. . . .

> This is the Cross—to become dead to the whole world; to suffer sorrows, temptations and other passions of Christ. In bearing this Cross with complete patience we imitate Christ's passion and thus glorify our God and Father as His sons in grace, co-heirs of Christ.[16]

St. Innocent on the Cross

In his marvelous little book, still to be properly translated into English, entitled *Indication of the Way to the Kingdom of Heaven*, Innocent, the enlightener of the Aleuts and the apostle to America who began as a married priest in Siberia and ended his life as the Metropolitan of Moscow, wrote specifically about the meaning of bearing the cross of Christ. He distinguishes between exterior crosses and interior crosses.

---

[16]Symeon the New Theologian, *Practical and Theological Precepts* 48, 107, 114.

He identifies the first as the unpleasant, painful, difficult and oppressive things that happen to us in our lives on earth; sickness, suffering, insults, tragedies, rejections, persecutions of various sorts, and ultimately the final cross of death. He calls interior crosses the sufferings that occur within people's souls as they struggle with their fallen condition in the world, with their passions and lusts, their vanities and prides, and with every spiritual trial and temptation, which is always rooted in sensuous self-love. It is this sort of crucifixion about which St. Paul speaks when he says that "the fruit of the Spirit is love, joy, peace, patience, kindness, goodness, faithfulness, gentleness, self-control ... and those who belong to Christ Jesus have crucified the flesh with its passions and desires" (Gal. 5:22-24). Innocent writes about it in this way:

> When the Lord is pleased to reveal to us the state of our souls, then we feel sharply that our hearts are corrupt and perverted, our souls are defiled and we are merely slaves of sin and passions which have mastered us and do not allow us to draw near to God. We see that even our supposed good deeds are all mixed up with sin and are not the fruit of true love, but are the products of various passions and circumstances ... and then we most certainly suffer ... in proportion as the Lord reveals to us the condition of our souls, our interior sufferings increase. .... But in whatever situation you may be, and in whatever suffering of the soul ... do not despair and do not think that the Lord has abandoned you. No! God will always be with you and will invisibly strengthen you even when it seems to you that you are on the very brink of perdition. God will never allow you to be tried and tempted more than He sees fit. Do not despair and do not be afraid. With full submission surrender totally to Him. Have patience and pray. God is our loving father. Even if He permits a person to fall into sin it is only in order to make him realize his own impotence, weakness and nothingness ... to teach him never to trust in himself and to show that he can

do nothing good without God. It is to heal his soul
that the Lord lays crosses on a person . . . to make him
like Jesus Christ . . . to perfectly purify his heart in
which He Himself wishes to dwell with His Son and
His Holy Spirit.[17]

The heart of every cross, interior or exterior, is the denial
of self for the sake of loving God and the brethren, a killing
of the sinful passions, a destruction of self-love and self-
will. This is the traditional "spirituality" of the Orthodox
Church. The entire sacramental life of the Church is only
about this. We are baptized and sealed with God's Spirit in
order to be "baptized with the baptism with which Christ is
baptized," which is to suffer with Him in order to live with
Him, to die to sin and to be continually born again to
righteousness, to put off the old Adam and to be clothed
with the new, who is Christ. It is, in the words once more of
the Apostle Paul, to "put to death what is earthly in you:
fornication, impurity, passion, evil desire and covetousness
which is idolatry" and to put on "as God's chosen ones, holy
and beloved, compassion, kindness, lowliness, meekness and
patience . . . and above all, to put on love which binds everything together in perfect harmony" (Col. 3:5-14).

Being baptized and sealed, we eat and drink the Lord's
broken body and shed blood at the table in His Kingdom
during the Divine Liturgy in order to bear His passion and
suffering in our lives, so that dying with Him we can live
with Him, and enduring with Him we can reign with Him
in the Kingdom which has no end. Communing with the
crucified, victorious Lord, we are anointed by the grace of
His Spirit so that our sufferings in the flesh can avail to the
salvation of our lives, and so that our very death can be, with
that of Christ crucified, unto the forgiveness of our sins, the
healing of our souls and bodies, and life everlasting.

Orthodox spiritual and sacramental life is a life lived not

---

[17]A translation of St. Innocent's work, entitled *An Indication of the Way
to the Kingdom of Heaven,* was made some years ago in Indiana, Pennsylvania
and is now out of print. SVS Press plans to publish the work in a second
volume to follow Paul Garrett's *St. Innocent: Apostle to America* (Crestwood,
N. Y.: SVS Press, 1979).

only under the cross, but *within* the cross. The supreme expression of God's mercy and kindness and love for man is that He enables His people to share in the sufferings of Christ and to be co-crucified with Him for the life of the world. It is man's dignity and glory that he has been blessed by God to bear the cross of his Master, in order to conquer the demons and bring joy to the world.

"Through the cross joy has entered the world"

This is proclaimed not only on the feast of the Exaltation of the Holy Cross. It is the festal hymn sung at the Vigil of every Lord's Day in the Church. It is the proclamation of the joy which is the essence of the Christian faith. The Lord Himself is "made perfect" through what He suffered (Heb. 5:7). And we are made perfect with Him in our sufferings for His sake, and with Him, for the sake of the brethren. We can "rejoice in our sufferings," as the Apostle writes, and our sufferings are ultimately our only source of rejoicing, for "suffering produces endurance, and endurance produces character, and character produces hope, and hope does not disappoint us, because God's love has been poured into our hearts through the Holy Spirit which has been given to us" (Rom. 5:3-5).

Genuine Orthodox spirituality is always a spirituality of the cross. When the tree of the cross is removed from the center of our lives we find ourselves cast out of paradise and deprived of the joy of communion with God. But when the cross remains planted in our hearts and exalted in our lives, we partake of the tree of life and delight in the fruits of the Spirit, by which we live forever with our Lord. Rejoice, O Lifegiving Cross!

CHAPTER 10

THE SYNTHESIS OF INTERPRETATION AND PROCLAMATION

How can Orthodoxy reach the heart of this nation if we continue to chew the past and speak to our youth in a language which they do not understand?

Metropolitan Philip

Paul Nadim Tarazi, who teaches Old Testament at St. Vladimir's Seminary, is one of the "new lights" arising out of the rebirth of the Patriarchate of Antioch. He prepared this chapter from the last of three special lectures given at Holy Cross School of Theology in Brookline, Mass. Fr. Tarazi is clear in stating that effective preaching to contemporary Christians needs the solid synthesis of interpretation and proclamation. In accomplishing this, the author reminds us that we must first familiarize ourselves with all the books of the Bible, and then, that we are called to be prophets and apostles according to the preaching of the early Church. Tarazi leads the reader through some of the most important concepts of becoming such an "apostle," as he discusses the kerygma, patristic preaching, and fatherhood. Resting on a solid theological basis, he finally reminds us that it is not only the preacher who, subjectively, preaches, but "the Word of the Lord which is uttered and that even he, the preacher, is part of the listening community."

J. J. A.

The Living Word
The Effective Preaching of God's Word Today

by

PAUL N. TARAZI

After considering the basic aspects of prophetic preaching, as found in the Old Testament, and of the Christian kerygma, there still remains the problem of *application*. This is, existentially speaking, the central issue for us.

Once we have studied the prophets and the Apostles, we are challenged to stop being spectators and to *act*. This entails a series of fundamental questions: Can we be prophets and/or apostles today? Is preaching, after all, a *real* issue in this present time? And if it is, how should we preach? And what should we preach? Now that God's Word has settled and somehow been limited in a series of texts we call the Scriptures, can we still speak of a living word or are we mere text interpreters? Do we always have to refer to the Scriptures when we preach? Is there any relationship between text interpretation and preaching? And if so, what is it? Assuming that the primary word of the prophets was effective and that of the Apostles had saving power, can we still say the same thing of our secondhand utterances today? Can our preaching today truly be the living word of God and His saving message, or is it, at best, a thorough reference to the Scriptures and a convincing invitation to read them?

These are some of the issues we ought to be tackling

now, and all of them relate to us personally—to our beings, our feelings, our behavior, our attitudes, our mission in life, and ultimately our faith in and commitment to Jesus Christ. There is, therefore, no need to explain, let alone prove, why this topic is a most delicate one. And for this reason, the reader must allow me to begin by immediately making two clarifications that will hopefully prevent misunderstandings or misinterpretations.

First of all, as we will be concentrating on the content rather than on the form of preaching, I must stress from the beginning that we would lose tremendously were we to think that the prophetic writings and the apostolic epistles are the *only* biblical books with any real bearing on our concerns in contemporary preaching. The historical books and their theology regarding God's deeds and economy, as well as the Wisdom literature and its place in this economy as an essential part in the preparation toward the fulfillment of God's plan in Jesus Christ, have much to say in the shaping of the preacher's mind. The same applies to the New Testament. How much impact would our proclamation lose if we ignored the creative works of Mark, Matthew, John, Luke, and the author of the Book of Revelation in our preaching? Let me then immediately make a statement to which I shall return later. *Close* familiarity with *all* of the biblical books is essential to the preacher of the living word!

Secondly, I consider the biblical canon as not merely a historical issue, but primarily a *theological* one. By declaring that the canon is *closed*, the Church confesses that Jesus Christ is the ultimate Logos of God and that in Him God's revelation comes to its end and goal. But since His *person* was central in that last divine message, consequently His death, resurrection, and exaltation, as well as the outpouring of the Spirit, were part of that ultimate Word and had to be included in that revelation through the word of specifically designated witnesses, namely the *Apostles.* We, preachers of today, must therefore be aware that our word is to proceed according to certain rules and between certain limits set once and for all by the apostolic preaching of the early Church. Our word should not be shaped by the whims of the moment, which we call "freedom," imagining that our fantasies, powerful as they might be, will be able to save the world. Rather, we must remember that our words, having been freed of the weight of sin, have become obedient servants of Jesus Christ (cf. Rom. 6:15-23), the one proclaimed by the Apostles, and only then will our words have the power to reflect the presence of the true and saving Lord. Let me conclude in trembling and fear: as preachers, our *thorough* familiarity with the New Testament books is not an interesting mental exercise, but a matter of life and death for our listeners!

This being said, allow me now to share with you some thoughts concerning the preaching of God's Word in our contemporary world. Needless to say, the following sketch is only selective and by no means exhaustive.

Kerygmatic Preaching

A primary question that comes to the preacher's mind is the following: Is the sermon only preaching, i.e., addressed specifically to the members of the community? Or does it also have to be kerygmatic, i.e., directed to outsiders, challenging them with the gospel and inviting them to have faith? Taking into consideration our immediate concern, I do not feel it is necessary to embark on a theoretical discussion of the matter. It would be more fruitful to approach the question from a practical point of view. The fact is that our congregations comprise people who have indeed adhered to Jesus Christ and who are conscious both mentally and practically of what faith is and requires. For such people the sermon is an exhortation to help them proceed on the blessed path they have chosen. On the other hand, a good part of our Church constituency is formed of *nominal* Orthodox, who know of the Christian faith but have never been actually challenged by the message of salvation. Such can be called the "in-outsiders." Added to this, our churches today may be attended throughout the whole Liturgy by nonbaptized individuals. All this means that the sermon is to be a springboard for a full kerygmatic message.

In the same line of thought, one must say that in every one of us there is that continuous struggle between the old and the new creation. In every sermon then, there should be an element of kerygmatic preaching to address the parts of our being not yet touched by the effects of baptism. A typical example of an exhortation to believers that is both preaching and kerygma is found in the Epistle to the Romans: "Do not, therefore, let sin rule your mortal body and make you obey its lusts; no more shall you offer the members of your body to sin as weapons for evil. Rather, offer yourselves to God as men who have come back from the dead to life, and your bodies to God as weapons for justice. Sin will no longer have power over you; you are now under grace, not under the law" (6:12-14).

As a practical consequence of the previous points, the preacher is to remember that what is assumed in his eyes has very often still to be proven to others. We preachers usually assume that God has wrought His salvation for us in Jesus Christ, that the latter is indeed the resurrected Lord, that the Church is His body, that we are citizens of God's kingdom . . . and like, in our sermons, to deal with the practical conclusions of those assumptions, trying to offer our hearers ways to implement their faith. But, by doing so, we forget that many of the listeners are, deep in their hearts, *still at odds with the basics of faith.* And if our word is to really reach them, it should be kerygmatic, that is, presenting them with the provoking experience of meeting God in action, Jesus in His actual Lordship, the Spirit in His effective power. It is then important for a preacher to challenge and stimulate *here and now* the faith of his parishioners, rather than their good works, so that both he and they are sure that the latter are indeed fruits of the former, and not just pharisaic exuberance.

I would even go further by saying that even if the preacher is dealing with an elite community where most of the members are aware of their faith, he should still preach, perhaps more often than not, *kerygmatically.* The reason is that taking our assumptions concerning God too seriously could be actually falling into the trap of taking Him for granted. As students of the prophets we must be aware that this trap is a real one: God too often becomes a known issue, an obvious topic, a familiar subject, a game whose rules we already know so well that we can foresee the moves—in one word, an idol, a toy in our hands. The preacher must understand the necessity of preaching *both to himself* and *to his community* in such a way as to face them with the loving but also living Lord, who is capable of convincing us that He is the true God by putting to shame and naught all our idols.

Confronting the Neighbor

One major, if not essential, aspect of the living God is His capacity to unveil the most intimate secrets of our hearts by meeting us in that face of reality which, more than anything else, receives the slightest vibrations of our inner being: *our fellow man*. Indeed, the other human being is the only feature in this universe that confronts us as a subject rather than bears our manipulations as an object. Indeed, he is the only one toward whom we can feel the whole series of nuances from love-passion to hatred-passion. He is the only creature that we cannot dismiss because he always pops up as an "I am" facing our "I am."

The human mind is able to conceive of our world without God—as witnessed in the case of many people past, present, and probably future. But no one can imagine it without *man*! Knowing this, God has precisely "clothed Himself" with every one of our neighbors. The prophets said it, Jesus affirmed it, and the Apostles proclaimed it: the neighbor is the criterion, the scale, the thermometer, our walking judgment, our practical sentence to either life or death, because God Himself is our neighbor. And the Bible is unequivocal about His choices: the powerless widow, the orphan, the poor, the meek, the wronged, the publican, the abject—in one word, the castout, those who have no place in earthly kingdoms. God made them citizens of *His* kingdom by taking abode in them.

The preacher is to face his hearers uncompromisingly with how the sins of overeating, lust, greed, egoism, pride, ex-

cessive richness, and individualism are opposed to God's Kingdom because they harm its citizens; they are opposed to Christ
because they crush all those whose faces and names He took
upon Himself. The preacher is to make his parish aware of
how our most intimate sins have a bearing on psychological
disturbances, social illnesses, and political horrors. He is to
stir up unrest in the hearts of his hearers until they understand that the body of the man left "half-dead on the way
between Jerusalem and Jericho" (Luke 10:30) is a potential
temple of the Holy Spirit, if not one already. He is to remind
them that they will not enter the Kingdom of God unless they
understand that the God to whom they have turned their
backs after the Divine Liturgy is the ἐρχόμενος, the One
who is eternally coming to us in every image of His: in our
fellow man, whose name we might know but perhaps more
often do not.

God took centuries to have the prophets conceive the inconceivable: Isaiah 53. God took another series of centuries
to realize and actualize that inconceivable in Jesus Christ,
the Son of man who has "nowhere to lay his head" (Luke
9:58). The preacher is not to undo what God has done!

Confronting the Total Christ

The Lord who faces us in the kerygma is our judge—a
loving judge, yes, but still judge of the most hidden corners
of our hearts. There, in those corners, everyone is somehow
a sinner, and the holy Lord cannot be approached but by the
holy. And the only way to holiness is *repentance—shûb*,
μετάνοια.

The preacher should never water down the issue of sin.
If the people do not understand it anymore, then he is to
teach, teach, and teach them that everyone of us—and there
are no exceptions according to St. Paul (Rom. 3:9-12)—is a
sinner somehow, somewhere, sometime. He is to explain to
them the different aspects and faces of sin by making them
almost feel it with their own fingers. Doing *only* that would
be pessimistic and ultimately destructive, and the preacher,

being rather realistic, is aware that recognition of our sins does not save us. However, he knows that, unless we do that, we shall not repent, and repentance is the key to God's Kingdom.

Jesus said: "People who are healthy do not need a doctor; sick people do. I have come to call sinners, not the righteous" (Mark 2:17). Only a sinner can be called to repentance. And unless the "righteous" unveils his secret sins, he will remain deaf to the call and will lose salvation. Repentance is thus the key word. The preacher must stir up unrest in the hearts of his hearers until they are turned over, returned, repented!

But how could one be *confronted* with all those things at the same time: sin, judgment, repentance, salvation, God's love, the Kingdom of Heaven? The answer is in Jesus Christ, the total Jesus Christ, His person. We know that the Lord is fully present in both the broken bread and the preached word. However, this "both-and" should not be understood as an "either-or." The latter understanding has led to two untenable aberrations: a eucharistic service without preaching, on the one hand, and a so-called independent Liturgy of the Word on the other. Only their combination is able to fully present us with Jesus Christ, Lord and Savior. Only their interrelationship keeps the former from becoming a mere ritual and the latter from being a mental exercise. Only he who has been faced with the power of the proclamation can be moved to be transformed by the Holy Spirit, together with his brothers and sisters, along with the offered bread into the one body of Christ, the new creation; and only he who has tasted the broken bread in the common cup can recognize whether it was indeed Jesus who has been preached or not. The word transforms the bread and the bread actualizes the word, and both confront us with the Lord Jesus of Nazareth, Judge and Savior.

In studying the apostolic proclamation we notice that the gospel is coextensive with the person of Jesus Christ. To say, however, that a person is himself the good news means that it is simply contradictory and impossible to imagine a preacher conveying the εὐαγγέλιον in bits and pieces in a series of sermons over a period of time. A person is offered in his entirety. Practically speaking, just as with every Gospel book, every apostolic epistle is a total εὐαγγέλιον, presenting not a part of Jesus Christ, but Him totally, only under a different light. And so every sermon—if it is meant to convey the good news—has to contain and convey the whole gospel.

Now the whole gospel for us is our salvation, our ultimate and complete salvation from both sin and death, which are the ultimate enemies of man (Rom. 5:12). Such an event was realized in the resurrection of Jesus from the dead, which meant their utter destruction, Christ proving Himself to be indeed the Victor and Lord. Let us hear St. Paul in his teaching about the resurrection:

> And if Christ was not raised, your faith is worthless; you are still in your sins . . . But as it is, Christ is now raised from the dead, the first fruits of those who have fallen asleep. Death came through a man; hence the resurrection of the dead comes through a man also. Just as in Adam all die, so in Christ all will come to life again, but each one in proper order: Christ the first fruits and then, at his coming, all those who belong to him . . . Christ must reign until God has put all enemies under his feet, and the last enemy to be destroyed is death . . . When the corruptible frame takes on incorruptibility and the mortal immortality, then will the saying of Scripture be fulfilled: "Death is swallowed up in victory." "O death, where is your victory? O death, where is your sting?" The sting of death is sin, and sin gets its power from the law. But thanks be to God who has given us the victory through our Lord Jesus Christ. (1 Cor. 15:17, 20-23, 25-26, 54-57)

Again, in the Apostle's beautiful summary of what the gospel is at the opening of his letter to the Romans, we read, "Paul, a servant of Christ Jesus, called to be an apostle and set apart to proclaim the gospel of God . . . concerning his Son, who was descended from David according to the flesh but was shown to be Son of God in power according to the spirit of holiness, by his resurrection from the dead: Jesus Christ our Lord" (1:1-4).

The resurrection of Jesus then is so central to the kerygma that it actually reflects the whole of the proclamation. The preacher should therefore be aware that, although the resurrection took place at the tomb near Jerusalem, both its presence and its effects cannot be limited to that place. St. Matthew tells us that the Apostles experienced it in Galilee (28:10, 16-20), while St. Luke reports in his Book of Acts that it faced Saul at the gates of Damascus (9:1-19; 22:5-16; 26:9-18). Said otherwise, it is not enough to refer to the resurrection—it is the preacher's duty to confront his hearers with it *now*. Our hearers must be confronted, through our plastic words, with Jesus Christ, pierced by the nails of our sins, and yet as the powerful and loving Master offering a helping hand to remove us from the quicksand of those same sins. It is the whole being of the resurrected Jesus *confronting* our whole beings and convincing us that we are capable of being resurrected.

After hearing our sermon, the listeners should be able to say—if I may combine Rom. 8:29, 34 and Gal. 3:1: "Jesus Christ, our eldest brother, was displayed before our eyes upon the cross. What say we? But he is risen!" And perhaps some of them will go on, saying: "If we allow the Spirit of Jesus, God's Son, to cry in us: Abba, Father! then it is the Spirit Himself who is giving witness with our spirit that we are children of God. But if we are children, we are heirs as well; heirs of God, heirs with Christ, *provided that* we suffer with Him so as to be glorified with Him" (cf. Rom. 8:15; Gal. 4:6; and Rom. 8:16-17).

A Proper View of Patristic Preaching

We said in the beginning of this presentation that the preacher ought to be careful to remain in the limits of the apostolic kerygma as it is found in the New Testament and that he should therefore have a thorough knowledge of the biblical books. This is precisely what the Church Fathers did.

However, such an attitude did not make them slaves of the biblical wording, but on the contrary, gave them both freedom and assurance in conveying God's Word to their contemporaries in terms and images that hit home. By doing this, they have proved to be real children of the Apostles, both earthen vessels for the same treasure (2 Cor. 4:7).

Instead of continuing this venerable living tradition, we, unfortunately more often than not, act like spoiled children born in a rich family where their share in that family's life consists of sitting in a lazy-boy chair enjoying the fruits of their forefathers' toil. We either paraphrase the biblical text or at best quote the Fathers, thinking that thus we are at least doing the job! The explanation we give is that we are "keeping the treasure." But precisely there lies our sin: to imagine that the earthen vessels are holding the treasure, while the truth in this case is that the treasure is holding the earthen vessels from falling apart. We ignore the Pauline text, which reads as follows: "This treasure we possess in earthen vessels to make it clear that its surpassing power comes from God and not from us. We are afflicted in every way possible, but we are not crushed; full of doubts, we never despair. We are persecuted but never abandoned; we are struck down but never destroyed. Continually we carry about in our bodies the dying of Jesus, so that in our bodies the life of Jesus may also be revealed" (2 Cor. 4:7-10).

Our study of the Church Fathers should not be done solely with the intention of knowing what they said about the Holy Scriptures and what they are telling us, but also—perhaps more importantly so—with an eye to *how* the Fathers read the Bible and *how* they arrived at saying what they said to *their* contemporaries. We must be able to study the Scriptures as they did and to proclaim Christ to *our* contemporaries with the same zeal they had. It is not enough for the preacher to boast about how well the Fathers knew the Bible; he should strive to know it as well and—if he can—even better! I imagine the Church Fathers would be sad if they heard that they have begotten campaign managers instead of children!

The Fathers must be for us the most vivid invitation to the study of those great proclaimers: the prophets and the

Apostles. It is there that we will find the face of our Lord in its pristine beauty, and after having met Him, be able to convey Him—even without quotations!—to our hungry and thirsty brothers and sisters. There, in the biblical text, is the truest, most historical, most lively, and most accurate icon of His. Unless we know intimately not some kind of ethereal Bible, but *our* Bible, the one we have at home, whose pages have turned black at the corners and even been torn by usage, then, vanity of vanities, all is vanity, we and the children whom the Lord has given us as parishioners!

But let me rather give way to that Antiochian Father, perhaps the prince of exegetes, and certainly one of the greatest preachers of the word. In his famous treatise *On the Priesthood*, St. John Chrysostom writes:

> Our present inquiry is not about dealings in wheat and barley, or oxen and sheep, or anything else of the kind. It concerns the very Body of Jesus. For the Church of Christ is Christ's own Body, according to St. Paul, and the man who is entrusted with it must train it to perfect health and incredible beauty, by unremitting vigilance to prevent the slightest spot or wrinkle or other blemish of that sort from marring its grace and loveliness. In short, he must make it worthy, as far as lies within human power, of that pure and blessed Head to which it is subjected.
>
> People who are keen for athletic fitness need doctors and trainers and a careful diet and continual exercise and any amount of other precautions. For the neglect of a small detail in these matters upsets and spoils the whole scheme. Then what about those whose vocation it is to look after this Body which has to contend, not against flesh and blood, but against the unseen powers? How can they keep it spotless and sound, unless they possess superhuman wisdom and fully understand the treatment suitable for the soul? Or do you not realize that that Body is liable to more diseases and attacks than this flesh of ours, and is infected more quickly and cured more slowly?

Doctors who treat the human body have discovered a multiplicity of drugs and various designs of instruments and appropriate forms of diet for the sick. And the character of the climate is often sufficient by itself to restore the patient's health. And sometimes a timely bout of sleep relieves the doctor of all trouble. But in the present case there is nothing like this to rely on. When all is said and done, there is only one means and only one method of treatment available, and that is teaching by word of mouth. That is the best instrument, the best diet, and the best climate. It takes the place of medicine and cautery and surgery. When we need to cauterize or cut, we must use this. Without it all else is useless. By it we rouse the soul's lethargy or reduce its inflammation, we remove excrescences and supply defects, and, in short, do everything which contributes to its health.[1]

What St. John Chrysostom is telling us is that since the incarnate Word is a living person, the preached word has to be multifaceted, in order to be able to address each of its hearers according to his own needs. However, such a stand on the preacher's part entails a great difficulty, if not an impossibility, on the practical level. For how could we, at the same time, in the same sermon, address ourselves powerfully to all our hearers, taking into consideration all the nuances of their personalities with specific problems? The key to a solution lies in understanding the term "word" in the text of St. John Chrysostom to include also the daily conversations the priest is to have with the people around him, be they Orthodox or heretics. That this was precisely his intention is, moreover, easily grasped when we read the rest of the treatise.

Spiritual Fatherhood and Preaching

When we discussed above the centrality of the neighbor

[1]St. John Chrysostom, On the Priesthood, tr. Graham Neville (Crestwood, N. Y.: SVS Press, 1977) 114-5.

in carrying the gospel, we spoke about going outside the church building and meeting the Lord we have just met in the Holy Liturgy—in other words, " a liturgy after the Liturgy." Here also we can speak of "a word after the Word." The preached word being Christ Himself, it is to be extended to cover the priest's daily intercourse with his parishioners. This is what our tradition calls "spiritual fatherhood."

I would like here to advocate not only the importance, but also the necessity of "spiritual fatherhood" in the Church. It is through personal talks and before the Lord's icon in the mystery of penance that we are able to help each one of our people implement the Word, i.e., Jesus Christ, in his life. If the preacher's word channels God working out His salvation and new creation, the word of the spiritual father channels God's care that the new creature is sustained in its growth from falling apart. If the preached word creates, the daily word sustains and brings to completion. Let us hear the Apostle Paul himself, perhaps the preacher of the word par excellence, telling the Thessalonians:

> On the contrary, while we were among you we were as gentle as any nursing mother fondling her little ones. So well disposed were we to you, in fact, that we wanted to share with you not only God's tidings, but our very lives, so dear had you become to us . . . You likewise know how we exhorted every one of you, as a father does his children—how we encouraged and pleaded with you to make your lives worthy of the God who calls you to his kingdom and glory. That is why we thank God constantly that in receiving his message from us you took it, not as the word of men, but as it truly is, the word of God, which is still doing its work in you who believe. (Thess. 2:7b-8, 11-13)

Concentrating only on the preached Word to the detriment of spiritual fatherhood would be laziness on our part, and not theology!

All the foregoing being understood, a question still remains: We are far from being like the Church Fathers, let alone Christ's Apostles. How can we be sure that, in preaching in the freedom of the Spirit, we are channeling indeed God's Word? What is the criterion for the correctness of our word?

In my eyes, looking for such a criterion is being already on the way of emptying God's Word of being *sui generis par excellence*. After having done *seriously* and *thoroughly* what was suggested in the previous points, we should not look for external criteria, least of all for the size of the crowds attracted by our preaching! The Lord has warned us: "and *many* false prophets will rise and they will mislead *many*" (Matt. 24:11). Others will be preaching along with us, many of them against us. Our parishioners will tell us: "We are lost! Both you and the other preachers contend that you are preaching God's Word and yet you and they are saying different, if not opposite things. We do not know whom to believe anymore!" Then, more than ever, we must persevere. At the time of the siege of Jerusalem by the Chaldeans, both Jeremiah and Hananiah were preaching, each contending that the other was the false prophet. The odds even were with the latter against the former. Yet both preached and it was God who vindicated! Like Jeremiah before Him, the Lord Jesus remained alone on Golgotha and God vindicated!

Do we consider ourselves greater than Jeremiah and Jesus Christ? Or are we actually looking to have it *easier* than they did? Our only way out is to preach and preach and preach—even against the angels and ourselves, like St. Paul (Gal. 1:8)—until our last breath, so that we may then be able to say with the Apostle, "I have fought the good fight, I have finished the race, I have kept the faith" (2 Tim. 4:7). Our *hope* is that when the Word—which left God to fulfill its mission—returns ultimately to its source, we shall have been among those who were located on its blessed course. *Hope* keeps us from playing the Almighty God and thus offers both us and our hearers all the chances to be saved by the Lord's Word! Is that not after all what the proclamation is all about—our salvation and that of our hearers?

Conclusion: The Fruit of the Proclamation

Last but not least, we come to a practical point. Starting with the truth that the core of the New Tesament message is the person of Jesus Christ and that His work was to initiate new life, many of us tend to conclude that deeds are much more essential than sermons and that these are but empty words without the former. "Enough preaching, good example is needed" is the general motto today, and Christians seem to be for it more than anyone else. I cannot but disagree essentially with such a stand. Good example is ultimately but a fruit, an outcome, a consequence. Anyone who considers Christian action salvific in fact distorts it by making out of it "works of the Law." That is pure pharisaism, which was the donwfall of ancient Israel and what Jesus and Paul attacked the most. Good example, like good deeds, cannot save—even more, it could become the cause of our damnation.

What is basically wrong with the general motto is its assumption that both Jesus Christ and His work are in the past tense, that He *was* what He *was* and we are asked to follow His example. Well, this is not the message of the New Testament. The apostolic proclamation is rather that Jesus is the exalted Lord addressing now as then His community and that He is the Head who initiates now as well as then any action in His body, the Church. Jesus the Lord acts with the full power of His Word which, now as then, heals, gives sight and hearing, resurrects, changes hearts and minds, makes out of the stones children of Abraham—in one word, works out salvation. And the serious preacher knows that from the pulpit it is the Word of the Lord—and not his word—which is uttered, and that even he, the preacher, is part of the listening community.

Consequently, the preacher should not give excessive heed to the people who keep repeating, "Why don't you do what you are preaching about? If you would only stop talking and start putting in practice some of what you're throwing at us!" Apart from a few exceptions, most of these people are not interested in what the preacher is actually doing; their main

goal is to subtract themselves from the challenge of God's
Word by eliminating one of its sources: the preached word.
By overlistening to their comments the preacher will fall into
the trap of starting to believe that those people will change
if they see him in a better light and forgetting that the most
they will do is to make of him, the preacher, their example
in life. And lo! as a blind man guiding another blind man,
they will both fall into a ditch! (Luke 6:39) The preacher
should know better; it is not by concentrating on his own betterment that his word will be reflecting more powerfully the
Word of God, but it is rather by concentrating on the *study*
of God's Word and by *proclaiming* it both to himself and
to his hearers that both he and they will improve in their deeds
and be justified, sanctified, and redeemed in Christ Jesus
(cf. 1 Cor. 1:30). According to St. Paul, it seems that God's
scale in deciding the matter of betterment is completely different from the human one. Sometimes, it even seems that
God allows the preacher to appear spiritually stationary in
his hearers' eyes for the purpose of promoting His salvation.
But let us listen to the Apostle himself:

> And even if I were to boast it would not be folly in
> me because I would only be telling the truth. But I
> refrain, lest anyone think more of me than what he
> sees in me or hears from my lips [perhaps, about me].
> As to the extraordinary revelations, in order that I
> might not become conceited I was given a thorn in the
> flesh, an angel of Satan to beat me and keep me from
> getting proud. Three times I begged the Lord that
> this might leave me. He said to me: "My grace is
> enough for you, for *in weakness power reaches per-
> fection.*" And so I willingly boast of my weakness in-
> stead, *that the power of Christ may rest upon me.*
> (2 Cor. 12:6-9)

Earlier in the same epistle the Apostle writes:

> ... this treasure we possess in earthen vessels to make
> it clear that *its surpassing power comes from God and
> not from us.* We are afflicted in every way possible,

but we are not crushed; full of doubts, we never despair. We are persecuted but never abandoned; we are struck down but never destroyed. Continually we carry about in our bodies the dying of Jesus, so that in our bodies the life of Jesus may also be revealed. While we live we are constantly being delivered to death for Jesus' sake, so that the life of Jesus may be revealed in our mortal flesh. *Death is at work in us, but life in you.* We have that spirit of faith of which the Scripture says: "Because I believed, I spoke out." *We believe and so we speak, knowing that he* who raised up the Lord Jesus *will* raise us up along with Jesus and *place both us and you in his presence.* Indeed, everything is ordered to your benefit, so that the grace bestowed in abundance may bring greater glory to God because they who give thanks are many. (2 Cor. 4:7-15)

Nor should the preacher give excessive heed to himself, saying: "How can I preach what I am not actually doing?" What a disaster it would be if the preacher kept his sermons within the limits of his own value! What a tiny area of spirituality he would be teaching if he limited himself to what he imagines his worth is! What a blasphemy it would be, since by thus doing he would be ultimately preaching himself! No, the preacher is not to concentrate on himself—he will do that before the Lord's icon, in the presence of his spiritual father, asking forgiveness in tears and humility, praying that God will keep this earthen vessel to be used for the greater glory of His name! But as preacher, he is to concentrate on God's Word, studying it, preparing his sermon in tears when the text is judging him, and—unworthy though he be—approach the pulpit as he would the chalice, and there speak out. He is to do all this so that not his voice but God's Word is heard, not his weakness but God's power is preached, while he— this time a listener of the Word together with his parishioners—is challenged by each word coming out of his own mouth! And both preacher and parishioners, heeding not their own thoughts and feelings but the Lord's Word, will grow into a living image of the Most High!

CHAPTER 11

A SYNTHESIS OF CHURCH
AND STATE

*Those who have no past, have no
present and will have no future. We
Orthodox, however, have a tendency
to always glorify the past and bask
in its glory. We seem to know so much
about the past, but so little about the
present, while the future is constantly
pressing upon us.*

Metropolitan Philip

John L. Boojamra, an Orthodox church historian, has come to be known for major contributions in two fields: history and education. Although his primary education, and therefore his first love and concern, is in the area of history, he has been a prolific writer and lecturer in Christian education, at times serving as a professor in both disciplines at St. Vladimir's Seminary. In this chapter, Prof. Boojamra deals with the synthesis of Church and state through two prominent historical figures: Constantine and Justinian. He makes his way easily through the complex fabric of Byzantine history spanning the reigns of the two emperors, and critically examines the changes that occurred in that period. In dealing with this particular synthesis, the author establishes the fact that ecclesiastical affairs were not isolated from the imperial and political life of the day. He does not fail to show both the positive and negative suppositions of this synthesis, from which the contemporary Church can even derive some direction.

J. J. A.

Constantine and Justinian

by

JOHN L. BOOJAMRA

With regard to the church-state synthesis, the historian, unlike the theologian, is confronted with the fact that there often is a *nonmutual* synthesis. This article is about one such nonmutual synthesis involving two different but crucial personalities in history: Constantine and Justinian.

No institution can develop to its full potential—at least as a free institution—in a heteronomous relationship of power. Such was the experience of the Church in the Byzantine empire. Throughout most of its history, the Byzantine Church confronted a friendly but immensely powerful state, with which it sought to establish a synthesis. This search for a synthesis, rooted in the belief that the polity could be "transformed," largely resulted in struggle. This struggle was, in turn, rooted in the deception that a common purpose could be defined for both the *imperium* and the *sacerdotium*.

Obviously, the growth of freedom and integrity is rendered more difficult in such a nonmutual situation. The Orthodox Church in Byzantium is precisely a case in point. It was forced to exercise constant vigilance in order to maintain the integrity of its faith in the face of imperial interference. It was no accident that the Church in Byzantium became stronger, assumed greater leadership, and refined its doctrine more clearly as the empire declined after the thirteenth century. However, the pattern of heteronomous relations had already been set by Constantine and Justinian, to whom we now turn.

Constantine

The conversion of Emperor Constantine initiated a series of events that, taken as a whole, set the pattern for ecclesiastical-imperial interaction for more than a thousand years! Constantine's relations with the bishops of the Church were in no way formally planned, occurring only within a general theory of "kingship" that was then being worked out as a synthesis of Roman, Christian, and Hellenistic principles. Neither Constantine nor the bishops had any *established* policy, or even a precedent for such a policy; they were, in a sense, playing their new association "by ear."

In a deeper sense, then, the purpose of this article is to examine the development of, and change in, the emperor's understanding of himself as *both* a Christian and an *imperator*. This, of course, will be seen through the synthesis worked out by Constantine and Justinian, and only passing reference will be made to the intervening two-hundred-year period.[1]

Without questioning Constantine's sincerity as a Christian, it seems apparent that he saw this new Christian faith as a foundation on which to rebuild the Roman empire after the chaos of the third century. To Constantine's mind, a truly cohesive society could only be achieved by fostering an identity of purpose among his people. He set about to establish this unity on the basis of the Christian faith and a revised theory of Roman imperial government. The Christian imperialism toward which Constantine was working, however, was not clear in all its implications until Justinian (527-565), who will be discussed in the second part of this article.

During the fourth century, for Christian and pagan alike, there was a common assumption of Roman imperial power, based on Hellenistic principles.[2] This conviction, along with the ever-more-prominent Christian religion, was to be the foundation for Constantine and his successors in their efforts to *consolidate* the empire.[3]

[1] See Francis Dvornik, *Early Christian and Byzantine Political Philosophy* 2 (Washington, D. C.: Dumbarton Oaks, 1966). Chapters 10, 11 and 12 constitute the best general introduction to this period.

[2] Ibid., p. 630.

[3] Dvornik has suggested that Christianity's monarchic principles made Constantine's transition to the new faith much easier. See ibid.

However, confusion is met when we look at Constantine's position and actions vis-à-vis the Church. This is primarily because of the inchoate nature of their association. That Constantine was uncertain of his position in ecclesiastical affairs is evident from the handling of the Donatist affair, as well as from the synods of Rome (313) and Arles (314). Similarly, Constantine's actions throughout his reign indicate his great discretion and caution in dealing with the yet significant pagan elements in the empire. He had no intention of committing the political suicide of an outright rejection of paganism and its cultic expressions. The ambiguity of the Sol Invictus cult certainly helped in this slow and cautious process of "transforming a pagan to a Christian empire." Justinian, by comparison, had no such limitations, and his clear and decisive actions in seizing control of ecclesiastical and theological events, opposing both pagans and heretics, was to a great extent the normal result of the development of "imperial self-confidence" over a period of two hundred years.

Before the conversion of Constantine there was no question about the relations of ecclesiastical structures of the Roman state; they were clearly *separate*, and all the Church could hope for was a benign toleration. The Church was consequently well aware of its institutional and theological independence.[4] Constantine's conversion came as a surprise, and necessitated a rethinking of the traditional relationship between the two institutions. The theory and practice that was to develop as a result was based on the synthesis of the three aforementioned influences—the Roman, the Christian, and the Hellenistic.

The Influence of Eusebius on the Synthesis. The Roman-Christian imperial theory and practice was shaped, to a great extent, by Christian writers. It must be remembered that the early Christians, even before the shock of the "conversion" of Constantine, tended under Pauline influence toward a *descending* theory of authority: all power comes from God,

---

[4]R. W. Carlyle and A. J. Carlyle, *A History of Medieval Political Thought in the West* 1 (London and Edinburgh, 1903) 176.

and not from the people! Indeed, it was a Christian—Eusebius of Caesarea, Constantine's historian and adviser—who was the originator of formal Christian imperial thought. Eusebius united the threads of Christian Scripture and tradition with the Hellenistic ideas of kingship and Roman caesaropapism, producing the fundamentals of Byzantine political philosophy.[5] We cannot but assume that Constantine was only too readily influenced by Eusebius in working out his imperial role in ecclesiastical affairs.

Eusebius' goal was simple: to make sense out of recent events as providential, and to justify a Christian society being coextensive and integrated with a transformed Roman empire. His purpose he performed well and enthusiastically. Earlier Christian writers, of course, had no need to do this. The Roman empire had merely been one, albeit superior, among the many pagan powers ordained by God.[6]

The historian Baynes, for one, is careful to point out that Eusebius' *Oration* on Constantine's tricennalia was a highly developed expression of a Christianized Hellenistic theory of kingship.[7] Seeking to fashion a theory of a Christian Roman empire, Eusebius readily seized on Hellenistic material already at hand. Indeed, only an easterner like Eusebius could have commanded the necessary thought categories of political Hellenism to achieve such a feat.[8] This Hellenistic undercurrent in Eusebius is clear from his many allusions to sun symbolism.[9] Furthermore, the classical Greek virtues of φιλανθρωπία (philanthropy) and εὐσέβεια (piety) appealed to his Christian predisposition (and were to survive as imperial ideals until the demise of the empire). Thus, in

[5]Deno Geanakoplos, "Church and State in the Byzantine Empire," *Church History* 34 (1965) 384. Geanakoplos provides a full discussion of the term "caesaropapism" and the difficulty of its application in describing Byzantine religio-political interaction.

[6]F. Edward Cranz, "Kingdom and Polity in Eusebius of Caesarea," *Harvard Theological Review* 45 (1952) 47. Augustine took a radically different approach: even Christian Rome was still seen as Babylon, and human society was viewed as a mixture of the "two cites."

[7]Norman Baynes, *Constantine the Great and the Christian Church* (London, 1932) 14.

[8]Dvornik, p. 614. Dvornik's point is that this is the only manner in which the development of Byzantine political philosophy can be understood.

[9]See Eusebius of Caesarea, *Vita Constantini* 1:43.

Eusebius, Constantine found a Christian thinker who was well schooled in Hellenistic thought and ready to find "not only God in the reflection of an earthly monarchy, but also the emperor in the reflection of the divine monarchy."[10]

For Eusebius, all authority, both secular and religious, was derived (descended) directly from God. The divine Logos, the incarnate Word, was the perfect nexus of both spheres of authority. After the resurrection and ascension, the two areas of responsibility were divided, the *spiritual* being assumed by the Apostles and their successors, and the *secular* being assumed by the Roman emperor. The Roman emperor is, therefore, the representative of Christ, the Χριστὸς Κυρίου. In virtue of this representative function, the emperor, in Eusebius' thought, derives his reason from the great Source of all reason, and maintained a unique fellowship with that perfect Source of wisdom, goodness, and righteousness.

Eusebius' *Oration* on Constantine's tricennalia is perhaps the most significant expression of this theory; after all, he had at least thirty years to develop it. Without making the emperor a god, he clearly states the case for the Hellenistic king: "His [Christ's] friend [the emperor] brings those whom he governs on earth to the only begotten word and Saviour and renders them fit subjects for his Kingdom."[11] The emperor is defined as the "friend of the Logos," and this immediate communication with the Godhead enables Eusebius to speak of the emperor as the source of all law.[12]

The *Oration on the Tricennalia*, moreover, clearly states the principle of "imitation" or parallelism. The emperor is called upon to govern his earthly kingdom according to the pattern of the divine, original monarchy in heaven, which is the archetype to which the earthly kingdom must refer as an image or shadow.[13] This is the context in which we should view Eusebius' emphasis on the primacy of φιλανθρωπία as an imperial virtue.[14] The empire is likewise an imitation (μί-

---

[10]Dvornik, p. 614.
[11]Eusebius of Caesarea, *Oration on Constantine's Tricennalia* 2:2.
[12]Ibid., section 5.
[13]See ibid., section 3.
[14]Ibid., section 2. On the centrality of philanthropy and the importance of the Hellenistic background, see Demetrios Constantelos, *Byzantine*

μησις) of the heavenly kingdom. Thus, there is ideally one emperor, appointed *by God*, to rule over one empire.

Eusebius carried his association of the imperial power with the divine original even further. In his *Demonstratio evangelica*, he related the divine monarchy to the *pax Augusti* and from there developed this parallelism.[15] The coming of Christ was accompanied (not by chance!) with the advent of *peace* through Roman order, imposed on the world under Augustus. Just as polyarchy and war are natural partners, so likewise are monarchy and peace. The former corresponded, for Eusebius, with polytheism, and the latter corresponded with the revelation of Christ.[16]

Any distinction between the Church and the empire allowed by Eusebius was purely temporary. Both the empire and the Church were images of the Kingdom of God, and Eusebius speaks as if, with the passing of time, they would merge into a unity.[17] Christian society on earth was destined to be a totality and a unity. Later, Augustine would, of course, take a radically different and more sober approach, in the face of the barbarian onslaught against the "God-protected empire."

Constantine's Military Victories and Relations with the Clergy. Thus, we see in a Christian writer of the fourth century the conviction that the establishment of the *pax Augusti* and the imperial power were ordained by God's wisdom and providence. In the minds of the Christian emperors and citizens, the foundation was established for Byzantine imperial Christian practice. Constantine was, no doubt, flattered by as well as convinced of his divine election and mission; the

Philanthropy and Social Welfare (New Brunswick, N. J.: Rutgers Byzantine Series, 1968) 45-7.

[15]Eusebius of Caesarea, *Demonstratio evangelica* 3:7. Eusebius quotes the letter of Melito of Sardis to the Emperor Antoninus Pius, in which Melito urges Antoninus to protect Christianity "which grew up with the empire and had its start under Augustus." For a discussion of Eusebius' place as a Christian historian see L. G. Patterson, *God and History in Early Christian Thought* (London: Adam and Charles Black, 1967) 76-82.

[16]Cranz, p. 55.

[17]Eusebius saw an image of the Kingdom of God in a meeting he describes at the imperial palace between Constantine and some bishops (*Vita* 3:15). Cf. Cranz, p. 64.

confidence of some sort of vague election can be seen as early as his march to Rome against the "tyrant" Maxentius. This conviction of his personal destiny and mission has led one writer to declare that: "Constantine really seems to have been above all a mystic."[18] While it may be an overstatement to refer to Constantine as a "mystic," his military victories over Maxentius and Licinius went a long way toward convincing him that he was favored by God. Furthermore, the special treatment he received from the enthusiastic bishops greatly enhanced the sense of privilege he felt within ecclesiastical structures.

Constantine was eager to believe the theories of Eusebius— a man whose thoughts were congenial to his—that both divine and human elements were interlocked in human society. As Piganiol writes: "Constantine's political activity is inseparable from his religious thought, so profound and sincere."[19] Perhaps it is in this sense that Constantine was a mystic, or, as some would suggest, superstitious. This element is quite clear in Constantine's letter to Anulinus, in which he granted immunity from public service to all the clergy on the premise that the state would benefit thereby.[20] The duties of the priesthood were seen as a full discharge of "civic" responsibility. Again, after the Council of Nicea, he wrote:

> Since it is proved to me from the prosperous state of the commonwealth how great the Almighty God's goodness has been to us, I thought I would bring it about that the saintly people of the catholic Church should preserve one faith, sincere charity, and a profound reverence for God.[21]

Thus, we see an essential principle of the Constantinian mentality: the good will of God was not unconditional, but a *function of proper imperial behavior*. It was the emperor's responsibility to maintain peace and concord in the Church

---

[18]L. Brehier and P. Batiffol, *Les survivance du culte imperiel romain* (Paris, 1920) 37.
[19]Andre Piganiol, *L'Empire chretien* (Paris, 1947) 33.
[20]See Eusebius of Caesarea, *Ecclesiastical History* 10:7.
[21]*Vita* 3:17.

of God. Consequently, Constantine acted against schism and heresy not only because they produced civil discord within the empire, but because they would rouse God's anger against the empire. And hence, at an early stage in church-state relations, schism and heresy became potentially illegal activities, subject to civil sanctions.

Constantine's part in this cosmic *do ut des* ("you do, so that I might do in return") relationship was fulfilled in many ways. For example, imperial legislation for Constantine (and later for Justinian) was inspired by Christian principles and a desire to effect these principles in practical life.[22] Eusebius lists numerous welfare activities initiated by Constantine, among them the regular corn distribution to each city for the purposes of episcopal charity.[23] In 321, eight years after the so-called *Edict of Milan*, Constantine granted numerous privileges to the Church, such as the right to receive bequests from individuals. A leading characteristic of Constantine's legislation— and one that will be more pronounced in that of later emperors, particularly Justinian—was the increasing integration of the ecclesiastical and the secular functions of the bishops. In fact, the most striking change that was taking place with the church-state synthesis was the extent to which ecclesiastical officials were called upon to assume local administrative functions.[24]

This approach to the Church is obvious in the letters and events associated with the Donatist controversy. The initial question in that controversy was raised by the imperial gift of money to be distributed to the catholic churches of North Africa by Anulinus, the governor. The next phase was the summoning of an imperial commission, headed by Miltiades, the bishop of Rome, to examine the protest of the group that would later be referred to as the "Donatists." Interestingly enough, Miltiades accepted this assignment to function as an

[22]On the Christian nature of this legislation, see Ernest Stein, *Histoire du Bas-Empire* 2 (Paris, 1949) 395-400.

[23]Theodosius II, *Code* (hereafter referred to as CT) 1.16.11. We use the edition prepared by C. Pharr for the Princeton University Press in 1952.

[24]This development was more significant in the West, where local civil government was severely disciplined due to the barbarian incursions. On this tendency see my article "Christian *Philanthropia:* A Study of Justinian's Welfare Policy and the Church," *Byzantine* 7 (1975) 345-73.

imperial agent, but then converted the commission into an ecclesiastical synod by inviting to it more than the original five bishops named by Constantine.[25]

Constantine, in his letter to Miltiades, made it clear that what was intolerable to him was that the West should be split into ecclesiastical factions. An imperial commission was the normal means of settling such questions in civil matters. However, the important point here is that he selected *bishops* to act as imperial or civil agents. He himself was probably unaware of the ecclesiastical synodal procedure; Bishop Miltiades simply reacted to the directive in ecclesiastical terms, calling a *synod* to investigate the matter.

That Constantine thus learned of ecclesiastical procedure is evident from the fact that the next stage in the Donatist affair was the calling of the Synod of Arles in May 314. But whatever form it took, Constantine's attempt to settle the affair for political reasons represented a departure both from practice and from the autonomy formerly enjoyed by the Church. The emperor took the initiative to solve an *essentially ecclesiastical* problem for *political* reasons!

It is not clear precisely how, at this early stage, Constantine saw his role in ecclesiastical affairs, or whether he even saw a distinction between the secular and the ecclesiastical. One thing, however, *was* clear—ecclesiastical affairs were *not* isolated from his other imperial concerns, but were intimately associated with all aspects of political life. On this basis, Constantine could justify his intervention in church affairs. His letter to Aelafius (314), informing the latter of the calling of the Synod of Arles and ordering him to provide the facilities of the public post to transport bishops to southern Gaul, reveals that he greatly feared the wrath of God against the human race should the Donatist affair not be settled. Once the affair is settled, he wrote:

> Then shall I be able to remain truly and most fully without anxiety, may always hope for all the most prosperous and excellent things from the ever-ready kindness of the most powerful God, when I shall

[25]*Vita* 3:17.

know that all, bound together in brotherly concord, adore the most holy God with the worship of the Catholic religion that is His due.[26]

Considering this direct and intimate association between the well-being of the empire and the harmony of the bishops, it is not difficult to conclude that Constantine saw the bishops as, in a certain sense, "imperial officials"—albeit officials with special theological functions. But neither after Arles nor after Nicea did Constantine consider himself a competent theological judge, and he fully accepted the episcopal decisions of the two assemblies. After the decision of Arles and its rejection by the Donatist faction, he wrote:

> They claim judgement from me, who am awaiting the judgement of Christ; for I declare, as is the truth, that the judgement of the bishops ought to be looked upon as if the Lord himself were sitting in judgement.[27]

From the text of this letter, addressed to the bishops still assembled at Arles, we can conclude that Constantine would have been happy to *let* the bishops settle the matter. If the Donatists had abided by the decision, there would have been no problem. But since they did not, Constantine threatened imperial coercion, in order to enforce civil peace in North Africa. Therefore, those who rejected Arles were to be sent to the imperial court.[28] St. Optatus, who compiled a history of the Donatist controversy along with a dossier of relevant documents, felt that it *was* within the emperor's competence to judge theological questions. The fourth-century conception of the divine role of the emperor was so strong that Optatus attacked the Donatists precisely on the basis of their rejection of the *imperial* command to conform to the decision of Arles. It is the Church, Optatus maintained, that is in the empire, not the empire that is in the Church.[29] Despite this

---

[26]Constantine, *Letter to Aelafius*, found in Optatus of Milevis, *Against the Donatists*, tr. O. R. Vassall-Philips (London, 1917) app. 3, p. 387.

[27]Constantine, *Letter to the Catholic Bishops*, in Optatus, app. 5, p. 396.

[28]Ibid., p. 397.

[29]Ibid., p. 132.

enthusiastic imperialism, however, it seems that had Optatus disagreed with the emperor, he would have violently opposed imperial intervention. As the Carlyles observe:

> We think that, while some of the Fathers use ambiguous phrases, there can be no serious doubt that after the conversion of Constantine, as much as before it, churchmen did normally refuse to recognize any authority of the civil ruler in spiritual matters.[30]

Without going into the further and quite interesting details of the Donatist question, we can at this point conclude that Constantine's role in ecclesiastical matters in the early fourth century was at least ambiguous.

The Example at Nicea. The events surrounding the Council of Nicea do not significantly alter this conclusion. Constantine, at this time, expressed the very same concern for the well-being of the empire out of fear of divine anger when he wrote to Alexander of Alexandria and Arius: if concord could be established among all of the Christian believers, the state would greatly benefit.[31]

In summoning the Council of Nicea, Constantine chose to accept the standard ecclesiastical pattern for such meetings. The location, significantly, was chosen for its proximity to the imperial residence and, hence, the influence of that residence. When it finally met, the council was, in a real sense, a *joint* meeting. It was summoned and presided over by Constantine, and followed, as was the Church's practice, Roman senatorial procedures. And yet it was entirely an ecclesiastical assembly: both senatorial procedure and church tradition denied the emperor a vote.[32]

Thus, the emperor, whose right to convoke and preside over a council was never questioned, could *de jure* only confirm the ecclesiastical decisions and promulgate them as law. In fact, the senatorial pattern of these meetings enables us

[30]Carlyle and Carlyle, pp. 175-6.

[31]*Vita* 2:64-72.

[32]On the structure of the church councils paralleling the senatorial pattern, see Baynes, p. 88.

to explain many of the difficulties that were previously characterized as evidence of "caesaropapism." There can be no doubt, after Arles and Nicea, that Constantine fully recognized the episcopal competence to decide theological matters. He wrote to the bishops who were not present at Nicea, for instance, that whatever the holy bishops decide in such a council is the divine will.[33]

The Eusebian phrase τὸν ἔκτον . . . ἐπίσκοπον[34] figures prominently in any atempt to define the relationship of the first Christian emperor to the Church. There are numerous explanations of this phrase, the most likely of which is that the bishops care for the *internal* life of the Church while the emperor cares for the Church as it *relates to society*. Another possibility is that Constantine saw his imperial function as including the conversion of pagans and heretics as well as the protection of Christians living outside the boundaries of the empire.[35] Whatever the proper interpretation is, however, it is clear that Constantine—as is particularly evident from the Council of Nicea—saw himself as having an integral function in the life of the Church. He saw himself as a type of universal "bishop," caring for the affairs of the universal Church.

Perhaps the most significant aspect of this new synthesis of the Church and the empire was the ascription of civil and secular functions to the bishops. Gibbon has pointed out that, while Diocletian and Constantine both separated the military and civil administration of the provinces, under Constantine a new order of ecclesiastical ministers, "always respectable, sometimes dangerous, was established in the Church and in the state."[36] The bishops, for example, were allowed to hear civil cases, and the formalities surrounding the legal release of slaves from their masters could be performed in a church instead of in a civil court, where the manumissions were

[33]*Vita* 3:20.
[34]*Vita* 4:24.
[35]Brehier and Batiffol, p. 37.
[36]Edward Gibbon, *The Triumph of Christendom in the Roman Empire*, ed. J. B. Bury (New York: Harper Torchbooks, 1958) 335. At the time of Constantine, Gibbon estimates that there were 1,800 bishops in the empire, 800 of them in the West.

previously performed.[37] The church building became a civil and judicial center.[38]

It was not Constantine's goal, then, to bring about any rapid or revolutionary change in the religious establishment of the empire. This conclusion will perhaps help to explain his many ambiguous measures. That his changes were designed to be slow and gradual can be seen from his relationship with the traditional imperial cult. By a series of measures, Constantine at first regulated the imperial cult for the pagan citizens—the cult was attenuated and remained sufficiently ambiguous for the sake of the majority of the population, which was yet pagan. Constantine did not forbid the erection of the imperial image and its veneration; he merely forbade its use in a temple or in a pagan rite.[39] And the inhabitants of Spellion in Umbria were permitted to build a temple to the gens Flavia and celebrate annual games in its honor, the only prohibition being that the temple not be spoiled by superstitious and idolatrous acts.

Thus, in spite of the fact that the old pagan imperial cult was partially rejected, it was being replaced by a new "imperial religion," in the words of Brehier:

All these facts suffice to show us the existence, in the Byzantine empire, of a firmly established monarchic religion, with its own dogmas, liturgy, and particular practices.[40]

This Christian imperial tradition was fixed for the next thousand years of Byzantine history and determined, positively or negatively, much of the direction of Orthodox church history during that period.

[37]CT 1.27.1; 4.7.1; 1.6.21; 2.5.7. This tendency increased greatly under Justinian. See Boojamra, pp. 359-71.

[38]Gregory Armstrong, "Imperial Church Building and Church-State Relations," *Church History* 36 (1967) 3.

[39]*Vita* 4:116.

[40]Brehier and Batiffol, p. 72.

Justinian

In spite of the bitterness of the Church's various conflicts with Constantine's successors, there was no radical change in the attitude of churchmen over the years toward the role of the emperor in church affairs. In fact, the legal proscription of heresy by Theodosius in the late fourth century was happily received by churchmen.[41] In general, however, we are able to detect a more cautious and restrained policy on the part of the Church with regard to imperial intervention. Still, this did not hinder the imperialist movement from reaching its acme under Justinian in the sixth century.

Justinian's views on his relationship to the Church cannot be separated from the fact that the overriding goal of his policies was the restoration of the greatness and geographical extent of the Roman empire. Indeed, an implied "Christian universalism" greatly stimulated his drive to reestablish the universal Roman empire.[42] Justinian's efforts to *control* the Church's ecclesiastical and theological life was a part of this restoration and reorganization of the empire. In terms of the control he was to exercise over the Church, he was the last "Roman" emperor to occupy the "Roman" throne.[43] The old ideas of Hellenistic kingship were still very much alive and had been reasserted in the face of new forces of independence in the Western Church since the Acacian schism.[44] As a result of the barbarian onslaught, the Church in the West developed a sense of independence next to an independent government organization. In the East, on the other hand, the Church was in close contact with a highly centralized and structured government organization, and there was no pos-

[41]Justinian, *Code* (hereafter referred to as CJ) 16.1.2; found in S. P. Scott, *The Civil Law* 12-15 (Cincinnati: Central Trust Co., 1932). On the key role of Theodosius I in the process of the legal establishment of the Church, see John L. Boojamra, "The Emperor Theodosius and the Legal Establishment of Christianity," *Byzantine* 9 (1977) 385-407.

[42]George Ostrogorsky, *History of the Byzantine State* (New Brunswick, N. J.: Rutgers Byzantine Series, 1969) 77.

[43]Ibid.

[44]Francis Dvornik, *Byzantium and the Roman Primacy* (New York: Fordham University Press, 1966) 71.

sibility for the conception of a free Church to arise until after the thirteenth century.

Justinian was certain of his role as *imperator.* The more he attempted to restore unity and greatness to the empire, the more he clung to traditional notions that Constantine had experimented with. Here we witness the same psychological elements. Justinian saw himself as the "elect of God," responsible for the unity, harmony, and correct doctrine of the Church. His legislation, more than that of any of his predecessors, is a clear example of Christian Hellenism taken seriously.[45] The empire was God's personal gift to him, and he wrote that he always had in "mind what concerns the needs and the glory of the republic which God has entrusted to us."[46] Justinian's views of himself as a Christian emperor were so clearly stated and put into effect that he in fact marks the beginning of a new political era.[47] This radical change is evident from his constitution of October 30, 529: the royal decision is absolute and applicable throughout the empire, and nothing is more sacred than the imperial majesty.

> Therefore, as we have found that a doubt existed in the ancient law as to whether a decision of the emperor should be regarded as law, we have come to the conclusion that this vain subtlety is not only contemptible, but should be suppressed.[48]

It was the *emperor,* in Justinian's view, who made and interpreted all law while being subject to none.[49] This was, in effect, the triumph of Hellenism as transformed by Christianity and codified in the *Codex Justinianus.*[50]

Justinian adhered to the Eusebian tenet that the emperor must *imitate* God's perfection. Nothing, he wrote, is more characteristic of the imperial majesty than humaneness, "by

[45]Dvornik, *Early Christian and Byzantine Political Philosophy*, p. 717.

[46]Justinian, *novella* 81; cf. also *novella* 148. The *Novellae* can be found in Scott, vols. 16-17.

[47]Dvornik, *Early Christian and Byzantine Political Philosophy*, p. 720.

[48]CJ 1.14.12.

[49]*Novella* 105.2.4.

[50]Dvornik, *Early Christian and Byzantine Political Philosophy*, p. 722.

which alone the imitation of God is effected."[51] The same point was made by the deacon Agapetus, in his admonition to Justinian (c. 530): God had given the scepter of power to Justinian, and he must model his rule after the Kingdom of God.[52]

Justinian took his responsibility as head of the Church more seriously than any other emperor. His object—which he pursued with more confidence and direction than had Constantine—was to identify the Church still more intimately with the *imperium*, blending them into a single organism over which he would have control. The Church was in no sense autonomous; popular church-state terminology cannot convey the religio-political structures of his reign. The more appropriate terms—*imperium* and *sacerdotium*—reflect the synthesis of two aspects in one empire. Justinian's great innovation in church-state relations was the unequivocal affirmation of imperial prerogatives in ecclesiastical affairs, and here the ideas of *imperium* and *sacerdotium*, rather than "church" and "state," become significant. The much overworked and equivocal term "caesaropapism" becomes meaningful with Justinian, and against this Justinianism the Orthodox Church would have to struggle until the end of the empire.

It is in the context just given that we must interpret Justinian's *novella* 6 (March 6, 535), perhaps the clearest expression of Justinian's Christian imperialism.

> The greatest gifts that God's heavenly φιλανθρωπία bestowed upon man are the *sacerdotium* and the *imperium*, of which the former serves divine matters, the latter presides and watches over human affairs, and both proceed from one and the same principle and regulate human life. Hence, nothing should claim the emperor's care as much as the saintliness of the priests, since these constantly pray to God for them [the emperors]. For if the priesthood is in every way blameless and acceptable to God, and the royal authority

[51]Cf. also *novella* 18.2.

[52]Agapetus, *Expositio capitum admonitiorum*. An English translation is found in Ernest Barker, *Social and Political Thought in Byzantium* (Oxford: Clarendon Press, 1961) ch. 12.

[βασιλεία] rules justly and properly over the state entrusted to it, good harmony will result which will bestow whatever is beneficial upon the human race.[53]

The Constantinian mentality was apparently very much alive in Justinian: the fear of divine displeasure was a fundamental concern of his in his efforts to achieve theological unity. The relationship between the two spheres of society was defined in ideal terms as a *synthesis*, but Justinian could not tolerate an independent Church, and did all in his power to control it both theologically and structurally.

Justinian's Intervention in Theology. Justinian's *novella* 6 made it clear that the moral purity of the clergy was a central concern of his. From the very first years of his reign he assumed administrative responsibilities formerly exercised by a synod. His zealous reform of ecclesiastical life was a necessary part of his God-given function of reforming the empire. He promulgated numerous laws to suppress simony and control ecclesiastical elections and the disciplinary and liturgical life of the monasteries.[54] The second section of *novella* 6, for example, established criteria for episcopal candidates and forbade bishops to absent themselves from their sees for more than a year without imperial permission.

In seeking to control the internal and theological life of the Church, Justinian went far beyond anything that Constantine could have imagined. In a decree of May 535 Justinian declared: "The priesthood and the *imperium* do not differ so very much, nor are sacred things so very different from those of public or common interest."[55] In effect, Justinian is saying, regardless of the twofold harmony posited in *novella* 6, the functions of the priesthood and its interests are not different from those of the *imperium*. Justinian thus reduces the function of the priesthood to that of interceding for the state.[56]

A theological preoccupation is evident from the very first pages of Justinian's Code, whose very first words are "Con-

---

[53]*Novella* 6. pref.
[54]Cf. CJ 1.3.41 of the year 528 and CJ 1.4.34 of 534.
[55]*Novella* 7.2.1.
[56]Dvornik, *Early Christian and Byzantine Political Philosophy*, p. 816.

cerning the most exalted Trinity and the catholic faith, and providing that no one shall dare to publicly oppose them . . ."[57] The very first title and chapter of the first book is the decree of the three emperors—Gratian, Valentinian, and Theodosius— of March 1, 379, proscribing heresy.[58] In *novella* 131.1 we find the decisions of the first four ecumenical councils and the injunctions of Holy Scripture set forth as imperial "law."

In implementing his duty as emperor, Justinian considered it within his competence to make and enforce theological statements. Such was the nature of his intervention in the infamous affair of the so-called "Three Chapters" and his well-received anti-Origen proclamation. Procopius, in his *History of the Wars*, describes Justinian burning the proverbial midnight oil in long and anxious conferences with theologians.[59] While we have seen how Constantine carefully avoided any such outright involvement, Justinian's *theological involvement* constituted his great *innovation* in the church-state synthesis.

Justinian's theological efforts were in general well received. None among the Orthodox opposed his edict of 553 on "One of the blessed Trinity was crucified"[60]—Pope John II praised it. Pope Vigilius—who was later to be the unhappy victim of Justinian's theological imperialism—thanked God on his ascension of the papal throne for having given Justinian both an imperial and a sacerdotal soul.[61] Opposition to his involvement broke out only on the question of the "Three Chapters." Justinian attempted, as he had done without episcopal opposition before, to issue a condemnation without a synod. Under ecclesiastical pressure, he in the end convoked a council, which gave him the decision he had wanted.

Justinian pursued his persecution of heresy with the same enthusiasm,[62] seeing his function as a Christian emperor in terms of proscribing *both* heresy and paganism. Symbolic of this was his closing in 529 of the Academy of Athens. The foundations laid by Constantine were fully developed by

[57]CJ 1. pref.
[58]CJ 1.1.1.
[59]Procopius, *History of the Wars* 7.32.9.
[60]CJ 1.1.8.
[61]Dvornik, *Byzantium and the Roman Primacy*, p. 75.
[62]See CJ 1.5.18.

Justinian. With typical exaggeration, Procopius informs us that Justinian:

> ... committed an inconceivable number of murders for the same cause: for his zeal to gather all men into one Christian doctrine, he recklessly killed all who dissented. ... For he did not call it homicide, when those who perished happened to be of a belief that was different from his own.[63]

All heretics and pagans were forbidden to teach any subject whatsoever.[64] Proper education was, no doubt, seen as essential to religious unity.

Finally, perhaps one of the most significant aspects of church-state relations—one already initiated by Constantine—was the increasing ascription of civil and civic responsibilities to the local bishop. In reinforcing the bonds between the Church and the imperial bureaucracy, Justinian not only gave the Church numerous benefits, but expected in return secular services from the local bishop.[65] This general process of legally assigning municipal duties to the bishops was an effort to regain control of rural and provincial areas through the bishops. Under Justinian this process was completed, and the local bishop became, in effect, the *defensores civitatis*. By a series of laws, the head of a diocese became the defender of the poor, the prisoner, the slave, and the victim of injustice.[66] The bishops, moreover, became responsible for public facilities and for overseeing the honesty and competency of public officials. Thus, the process of rendering the episcopal agent a civil servant was apparently complete.

Conclusion

From the foregoing examination of the relationship be-

[63]Procopius, *Secret History*, tr. Richard Atwater (Ann Arbor: University of Michigan Press, 1966) ch. 25.
[64]CJ 1.5.18; CJ 1.11.10.
[65]Stein, p. 399. See especially Boojamra, "Christian *Philanthropia*," passim.
[66]CJ 1.4.27-28 and *novella* 86.

tween the *imperium* and the *sacerdotium* in the political
ideology of Constantine and Justinian, we must conclude that
the synthesis that was effected was to the disadvantage of
the Church, especially in the East. She had, after Constantine,
to struggle to maintain her internal and theological freedom.

There was a gradual development in imperial self-confidence and self-consciousness from Constantine to Justinian.
This development was not to any great extent marked by
radical changes. However, the "normal" extent of this development was so great that with Justinian we see imperial
self-confidence at a point where the church-state synthesis is
qualitatively altered. The emperor, in Justinian's view, had
the full right to decide and legislate theological and doctrinal
questions without reference to the bishops or a synod. No
such possibility had ever occurred to Constantine.

This close association between the state and the Church
occurred on several levels. One was the proscription of heresy
and paganism, which began cautiously with Constantine's
ambiguous policy with regard to the Donatists. The policy
continued in legal terms with both Theodosius and Justinian.
We have already seen how the imperial self-confidence in
dealing with dissent changed from Constantine to Justinian.
Another level was the affirmation of Orthodoxy as law. And
finally, there was the control of the internal structure of the
Church.

This rapprochement of the persecuted Church of the
crucified Savior with the universal Roman empire was not a
historical necessity. However, it did occur, and the shape this
synthesis took between 313 and 565 was a two-edged sword
of imperial *support* and *protection* on the one hand, and
control on the other. Churchmen had enthusiastically sought
to permeate the political commonwealth with Christian principles and produce a new social order. Such was the ideal.
But it could not be achieved in a nonmutual setting. The
Church expended much energy during the same thousand years
of Byzantine history simply fighting off the efforts of various
emperors to deny her freedom to determine who and what
she is, and to define her experience of her Lord. The world
and its political and social structures *must* be the object of

the Church's witness; but each generation of churchmen must determine how best to do this, without sacrificing the mutuality that is a necessary aspect of her freedom to function in a "foreign" world.

CHAPTER 12

A SYNTHESIS OF PERSONAL WHOLENESS

Shall we surrender to despair, or is there hope for a better world? I am not a pessimist, nor shall I ever surrender to despair, for my Church is a church of hope. Despite the thickness of the clouds, the sun can still brightly shine. If you study the life of Christ, you will discover moments of sadness and moments of joy. This is how I understand history. The Church never promises us a paradise on earth. Therefore, we must reject all social utopian thinking, and accept both the blind and bright moments in history with faith, hope, dignity, and courage.

Metropolitan Philip

If there is one area around which so much misunderstanding exists, it is in the area of the Christian life and healing. This chapter attempts to deal with this question in a straightforward and Orthodox perspective. What is the connection between faith and healing? How does the Church practice healing? What place does the Orthodox pastor have in such an act? These and many other relevant questions are addressed in this chapter, which seeks to demonstrate that, in a proper view of healing in the Christian life, the synthesis of God's concern and man's response is realized.

J. J. A.

God's Concern and Man's Response in Healing

by

JOSEPH J. ALLEN

This article is an attempt at presenting certain pastoral aspects of personal wholeness (healing). It is a presentation of limited scope, a type of "working paper" which hopes to open new doors for the further study of pastoral healing in an Orthodox perspective.

The *first* limitation of its scope is the fact that it necessarily concentrates on aspects of *personal* healing, whereas other areas, such as "marital healing," "healing of the aged," "healing of the emotionally disturbed," etc., need a separate study, and one with quite a different "bias." This study will address itself then, as far as possible, to those key personal elements with which pastoral theology must deal. The *second* limitation of its scope comes as we note that it is a "pastoral" study. This is true because upon exploration into the area of healing, I discovered that it can be approached from the various perspectives of the various disciplines. One could view, for example, healing in a historical perspective, e.g., the history of healing; from a systematic perspective, e.g., the relationship of sin to disease; or from a scriptural perspective, e.g., the healing miracles of Christ, etc. Obviously, no area can be completely isolated from the other, but each approaches criteria and challenges with its own "eye." My "eye" will be a pastoral one.

Healing, like sustaining, guiding and reconciling, is one

213

of the key dimensions of pastoral theology.[1] It has to do with restoring a person to "wholeness," to an "integral unity." To be restored to such wholeness requires that something be "overcome," "cast out," "eliminated," "destroyed," as a possibility which blocks or stifles that wholeness. Without this wholeness, we have disease (ἀσθένεια)—or "dis-ease"— which is to say, not being together, not being "at ease" with one's life. To have this wholeness is to have, in a special way, "holiness" (both of which are derived from ὅλος), since holiness can also be described by the term "together."

One can see, from the very beginning, that such a definition cannot be the popular and "reduced" one in which one has an ailment, receives medication, and gets well. There *is* a connection, as this presentation will demonstrate, but it is at a much deeper level than such a medical model.

In order to further explicate this meaning of healing in a pastoral perspective, this presentation will proceed according to three distinct concerns: (1) the problem of linkage, or interpreting healing; (2) the praxis of healing; and (3) the pastor as a source of healing.

The Problem of Linkage: Interpreting Healing

We can begin by asking the question of "linkage" between faith and healing. Are they related, and if so, *how* are they related? How far does our theological understanding of man help us to interpret man's struggle with disease, both physical and otherwise? Persons have always asked: is the person who knows himself to be saved by the act of God in Jesus Christ and the Holy Spirit better able to solve his problems in terms of healing than one who does not know himself to be saved? Where is the line of delineation between where one is to attempt to actively solve his problems and, on the other hand, to "live with them"?

First, there is a "linkage" of faith and healing found in

[1] I have, in another place, called these four the pastoral "screen" through which all of our praxis must pass. They can be found in another form in Clebsh and Jaekle's *Pastoral Care in Historical Perspective* (Englewood Cliffs, N.J.: Prentice-Hall, 1964). See my article above, pp. 105-6.

Scripture itself, and we should begin there. "Scripture appears to take a double attitude toward the healing of disease. God is concerned with the health of man and . . . brings healing. At the same time, the biblical man of faith looks beyond present suffering, and assumes a certain indifference . . . as he anticipates a final fulfillment."[2] With this quote Daniel Williams describes the area in which we are considering the problem of healing: how God is concerned with healing, and how the man of faith is to respond to suffering.

This "linkage," found throughout Scripture, is shown as the language of salvation and the language of healing are interwoven. Furthermore, this linkage is often both a *causal* and *symbolic* one. In the Old Testament, God seems to be, at once, causer and healer: "disease and sickness come from the hand of God, as do all the fortunes and circumstances of life."[3] Here there seems to be a literal and physical linkage. Among the many examples (of which I found approximately forty!) we can take Deuteronomy, which says "See now that I, even I, am He, and there is no god with me: I kill and I make alive; I wound and I heal" (32:39). In Hosea we find: "for He hath torn and He will heal; He hath smitten and He will bind us up" (6:1). Later in Hosea: "Woe unto them! for they have fled from me: destruction unto them!" (7:13) Psalm 103 speaks of forgiveness and healing in the same verse: "Who forgives all thine iniquities; who heals all thy diseases" (103:3). When God "heals" Israel, whether seen as a causal or symbolic event, it seems to relate to His desire to lead them to salvation.

In the New Testament there is also a "linkage" of faith and healing, again both causal and symbolic. At every point, the healing of a person is transmuted into a question of faith and salvation. In Mark 5:34 we read: "Daughter, your faith has made you well, go in peace, and be made 'whole.' " This is also found in Luke 8:48, but now it is applied to the daughter who is dead: "Fear not, only believe and she shall be made 'whole.' " There are, of course, many more examples which

[2]Daniel Williams, *The Minister and Care of the Soul* (New York: Harper and Row, 1961) 14.
[3]Ibid.

the exegete could better reveal. In the New Testament one author has found *sixteen* examples of deliverance from disease and demonic possession, and over *forty* of deliverance from physical death.[4] The point, however, is that the healing of each somatic disease and suffering is related to the deliverance by, and presence of, God in Christ, and the healing of all of life through the restoration of the cosmos—i.e., it is related to the ultimate *meaning* of life. Again, in the New Testament the linkage is, at once, causal and symbolic. Thus, Jesus sends His disciples "to preach the Kingdom of God, and to heal the sick" (Luke 9:2).

In what way, then, can this scriptural "linkage" of faith and healing (wholeness) apply to the pastoral dimension of healing? How can we interpret such linkage in the contemporary scheme of things? Obviously, how we *interpret* the human experience is itself *part* of that experience.

To begin with, there are some obvious understandings in which we must place this contemporary linkage, so that we are not trapped in "magic" and misunderstanding:

(1) As has been said, the healings which were realized by our Lord Jesus Christ manifest the Kingdom of God in our midst, and the linkage is obvious.

(2) All healing can be causally and symbolically linked with the *act of God*, even though mediated through human resources and elements (which God created). However, *suffering* and *disease*, unlike healing, *cannot* easily be seen as the *act of God*, i.e., they cannot be seen in the narrow causal sense. For example, I recently heard one Orthodox priest say that a person (a child!) died because he sinned. (To relate "sin and death" is indeed the heart of the matter, but it must be seen in the universal sense, and certainly the homily, unless most carefully worded, is hardly the place to proclaim it!) Perhaps we could apply here the words of St. John's Gospel: " 'Who did sin, Rabbi, this man or his parents?' Jesus replied, 'Neither did this man sin, nor his parents' " (9:2-3). Thus, disease must be seen not in the narrow sense, but as sin and disorder which have broken in upon the world. After all, if

[4]H. Wheeler Robinson, *Redemption and Revelation* (New York: Harper and Brothers, 1942) 232.

we attempt such a direct relationship in terms of disease and sin, would we not be like Job's friend, who tried to make such a causal linkage: "Who ever perished, being innocent?" (Job 4:7) We can well understand Job's vehemence: "Ye are all physicians of no value!" (13:4)

(3) Faith is no guarantee, nor promises to be, nor is dependent upon, either our *somatic healing* or *suffering*. In the narrow sense of suffering and healing, one may suffer *more* because of his faith. Were we to be relieved of such suffering, then Christ, the martyrs, and all those "made perfect in faith" would not themselves have suffered. For the Christian, it may be a case not of "Shall I suffer or not," but rather *"How* shall I suffer when it is given to me?"

(4) As the antithesis, a person who seems to have done evil may even seem to be "more prosperous" in this life. Psalm 73:3 speaks of the "prosperity of the wicked," and Jeremiah asks: "wherefore doth the way of the wicked prosper?" (12:1) In the New Testament, we find in Matthew: "Your Father . . . maketh his sun to rise on the evil and the good, and sendeth rain on the just and the unjust" (5:45).

(5) In the Church, we pray and anoint the sick "unto the healing of body and soul." This shows an obvious linkage, alluded to earlier, in both the *cosmic* and the *individual* sense; the healing of the individual is a reflection of the healing of all life in the resurrection. We do, however, pray and anoint a particular body and soul, a particular individual, with a particular malady.

(6) Disease comes to man because, as St. John Chrysostom aptly notes, everything is liable to its connatural evil and malady, e.g., corn to mildew, wood to rot, body to disease. Here enters sin as disease and death in the causal sense! A disorder proper to man is touched by an outside evil, like spoiled or poisoned food touching that part of the body that will react to that bad food. One's soul, however, *if* it is exempt from evil, cannot be affected by an outside evil. In other words, we can *do* something about what is *in* us. Here enters the patristic insistence on ἀγαθὸν (the good) and ἀρετὴ (virtue). Why was Adam mastered by evil but not Job—

particularly since Adam was given everything? Similarly, Joseph's brothers injured him, yet he was *not* injured.

(7) Pain, as C. S. Lewis well notes, is a "megaphone of God"! When I am in pain, my brain tells me that something is wrong, and I scream. In a larger sense, suffering is a "scream" that something is wrong with our world, that we need help, that "there is *no* man who lives and sins not, and *Thou* only art without sin" ("without sin" meaning whole, perfect), and that only this megaphone can bring us to our knees. Our hope, we learn, is that "What is not assumed cannot be saved" (St. Gregory of Nazianzen). Christ assumed our mortality, and is thus our hope in immortality.

These are some of the crucial aspects of the linkage of faith and healing, of which the contemporary pastor must be aware.

The Praxis of Healing

Understanding the problems of "linkage" in both the scriptural and contemporary realms, however, still does not tell us what is involved in the praxis of pastoral healing. This is our present task.

As indicated earlier, "pastoral" healing is a veritable "spiritual" endeavor. Since "spiritual" (πνευματικὸς) is not opposed to "material," but indicates all that one *is* (*existential*) and *can do* (*teleological*), it may and should include both *physical* implications and *volitional-emotional* implications.

We can easily enough understand the volitional-emotional implications; the physical is another matter. To make this clear, we can take the example of a man with a *withered* hand (physical): he has the "spiritual" problem of what he will *make* of it, i.e., either his faith (toward God) or his bitterness (away from God) may increase. Is this not a case of "antecedent faith" in which the event is interpreted by the faith? Can this be what Jesus meant in Mark: "He that hath, to him shall be given: and he that hath not, from him shall be taken away even that which he hath" (4:25). We see here that the fundamental task for the pastor is still one of "faith," which meets and interprets the events of life.

Thus, when the physical dimension *is* involved, our prayer must be not only for healing in the narrow sense, but also for finding *meaning* in that physical disease; this is true, even though we pray and anoint for a *cure* of the ailment. In short, whether or not a physical cure comes, we still pray for and anoint the person. (Do we not see here that anointing has also a "consecratory" aspect?) Furthermore, at this point the paradigm of Lazarus also speaks: Lazarus was healed, physically being raised from the dead, but he still had to die. Pastoral healing, then, *includes but can never be limited to* the somatic cure of an ailment. This point is absolutely crucial for understanding the direction of the remainder of this study—and for understanding what is truly meant by "pastoral" healing. This *must* be said here, because the reader should look for neither a "cheap" understanding of healing, e.g., in the sense of a magical or "charismatic" raising of the dead, nor for any medicinal perspective of "healing." As previously mentioned, to focus on these aspects of healing would indeed require another type of study.

Healing and Human Experience. What then of the pastor's role in healing? Here we again can see his activity in the healing of another person as a type of "linkage." In terms of human experience, "healing" means to reconcile, i.e., to "link" each of these experiences with the larger questions of meaning. This he does as he leads another to discover that in the middle of my *problem* can be the meaning of my *existence*. "Wherever we begin with human problems we recognize that what we see and feel here and now, may *break open* for us at any time questions concerning the meaning of our existence."[5] The introduction of one's relationship with God, i.e., "the meaning of our existence," into the search for personal healing is not arbitrary, but is its very foundation. Healing does not, fortunately, always depend upon our understanding of its sources; it is God who heals regardless of the consciousness of the mediator. This, of course, the Orthodox priest must proclaim continuously. To see this is to see how

[5]Williams, p. 61.

God's grace works in healing—and it can be seen in the most fundamental situation.

This is true because man is both "whole and parts," his whole life, as well as his arms, his legs, his stomach; every part of his life and experience is connected with every other part. There is no incident in his personal history that may not be reflected in the direction of his whole being. Have we not seen this many times in history? "A trivial incident may open the way for the first time to the discovery of one-self and God."[6] Can this be what St. Paul means: "for our light affliction, which is for the *moment*, works for us more and more exceedingly an *eternal* weight of glory" (2 Cor. 4:17). An illness may become the only way that we face the ultimate issues of life. The struggle with ourselves (with our hate, revenge, anger—with our sin!) in all our relation-ships in which, for example, reconciliation finally occurs with another person, may bring into clear focus how we must struggle for reconciliation with God. Somatically, a *recovery* from an illness can reflect the goodness of God. These are all examples of "healing" as the reconciliation of our present experience with the meaning of our existence. Of course, one can never know beforehand exactly when this type of "link-age," i.e., of the part to the whole, will take place. But each incident may precisely lead someone to face those issues that go to the roots of his life, and it is this possibility which the pastor must keep alive for another person.

Furthermore, he must keep this possibility alive even in the face of those human limitations that may *never* be re-moved from the person's life. The real healing, in fact, may come just at that point where such limitations are acknowl-edged and are integrated into that person's courageous ac-ceptance. "The Lord gives and takes away; blessed be the name of the Lord" (Job 1:21). The limitation, whatever it be, may be that door through which one walks into the arena where ultimate questions are asked and answered.

Each situation we can present, then, can be an example of how the disease or suffering *itself* can be used to "heal." Here the prayer of Pascal makes real sense: "Thou did give me health that I may serve Thee, and I put it all to worldly use. Now Thou sendest me sickness to correct me; let me not use it to avoid Thee through my impatience."[7] Other *meanings*, then, besides the immediate ones must be discovered if the pastor will effectively "heal." Such a meaning must be seen as a new possibility for "linkage."

Healing and Other Selves. What does the pastor bring to other "selves"? What does his relationship to other individuals *mean* in terms of healing?

Every person has a way of seeing himself in relation to others, a "self-image." "Who am I" in relationship to God, other humans, the world? This self-image includes our feeling about ourselves, as well as other persons' feelings about ourselves. What is our role, our capacity, our direction? No one should pretend that this self-image does not bear a most heavy emotional weight; threats to our self-image are threats to our very being. Whether or not this should be the case, the problem here is that it is a fact. Our being itself includes our self-image, our self-interpretation.

One of the most important things that could happen when a person comes to the pastor is that person getting his self-image out before himself, thereby seeing it for what it truly is: self-interpretation through other-interpretation. What is false and sinful in our self-image, what is grandiose, prideful? Where is the discrepancy between what we *are* and what we pretend to be? Then again, when do we slothfully become "satisfied," forgetting that we are never totally defined by what we are, but by what we desire to become?

Here the role of the pastor is obvious. He is someone I trust, to whom I can disclose my "self" with all my sins. And, of all things, he represents God and the Church! When we talk with him (and I do not mean here only in the sacrament of confession, which can begin this talk but not limit it) we can hear what we are *saying*. Furthermore, he can help us to *interpret* what we are really saying. What "idols" have we created in order to avoid coming to grips with ourselves? What "idols" have we created that keep us from the painful

[7]Cited in Paul Tournier, *A Doctor's Casebook in the Light of the Bible* (New York: Harper and Row, 1976) 201.

truth about what is truly required in order for us to "co-operate" (synergy) with God? What is needed for healing in each case is a *reordering of our self-image*—and it must be a constant reordering (which means in turn, a continuing growth). This very personal relationship and communion can *release* a person and lead to such "healing."

The pastor can also help another realize that "the self-image is never *only* a self-image."[8] Immanence and transcendence can never be separated. We know who we are when we discover to Whom we belong. "It is not I who live, but Christ who lives in me" (Gal. 2:20). Can there ever be a self-understanding apart from some grasp of origin and destiny?

It is the pastor, then, who can best represent that world with which the person must come to terms, i.e., who can bear the truth about life which must be grasped. To lose *this* capacity is to lose everything! The pastor cannot afford to neglect this important task of healing. In a sense, he introduces the person to himself.

Healing through Inner Resources and Acceptance. But as we reflect on the healing of other selves, we must consider the problem of both the inner resources of man and the atmosphere in which those resources can be activated. Our consideration of these problems can begin with certain of the Fathers, e.g., St. Gregory of Nyssa and St. John of Damascus (also Nazianzus in *Oration* 45). Both speak about the growth and development of man "into Christ," which is his "natural inclination" (in the *Life of Moses* and *De fide*, respectively). Man *will* grow undeviated to where he *belongs*, to where he is most himself, unless he gets blocked by sin. (For the Damascene man is even "sinless by nature," sinning only by choice.) We must remove the "rust from the steel" to see its shine (Damascene) and the "athlete must throw off all undue weight" to compete (Nyssa). This means that the human already has *resources within himself* (via the potential given in the *imago Dei*) for appropriate

[8]Williams, p. 64.

direction. The problem is that sometimes he cannot *find* those resources. Here again enters the pastor.

In a pastoral perspective, we *can* speak of self-help without Pelagianism, because the self-help in which one discovers those resources is always forthcoming from *other*-help. But no other—not even God Himself—will do our part *for* us, and neither can the pastor. Here again the "medicinal model" breaks down. We cannot simply administer the medicine and healing occurs; the person's will, capacity, and choice is involved! The pastor cannot *force* such healing; he can merely help the person to clear the way, that is, to open himself to the grace of God which heals.

But more exactly, how can we as pastors help another to "help himself," that is, to expand his capacity to be open to God's grace? We can begin to do this by attempting to enter the sufferer's frame of reference, empathetically participating with him in his struggle, clarifying his thoughts, directing his attention properly; in this way we are more shepherd than "sheriff." "If the helping task is principally that of entering into the internal dialogue of the individual, standing in his shoes, clarifying his self-understanding... the sensitive pastor using such an approach can do little harm and much good."[9]

This is the atmosphere of *acceptance*. It is not approval. It is acceptance. This acceptance of another, even of the sinner, can be painful also to the pastor; he must leave space for the other; he must, in a sense, "die." Can our model not be found in Romans: "God showed his love for us in that while we were yet sinners, Christ died for us" (5:8). In this atmosphere—indeed, of the father who runs out to accept the prodigal while not *approving* of what he has done—the priest is able to communicate his own willingness, not only to enter with this person on his journey, but also to stand *between* the person and God as one who makes God *personal and available*. (Is this not the meaning of the Christ-event as it is lived in a present experience?) The new life in Christ, or rather the "healing," is the discovery of a new self on the

[9]Thomas Oden, *Kerygma and Counseling* (New York: Harper and Row, 1978) 36.

other side of an old existence which must be let go. "Purge out therefore the old leaven, that ye may be a new lump" (1 Cor. 5-7).

This is not easily done; self-disclosure *is* a death. The pastor, like the Church, offers no easy way out, since sin cannot be circumvented. But if one must surrender, and *this* is the point, the best place to do that is in that atmosphere in which we know we will be accepted.

Here I believe Jourard has captured what this can mean practically: "You can truly know me only if I let you; only if I *want* you to know me."[10] And further, "If he does not *wish* to tell us of his self, we can torture him, browbeat him, tempt him . . . but unless he wishes to make his self known we will of course never know it!"[11]

It is only in this atmosphere of acceptance that one can, in a sense, "objectify" himself, i.e., he comes to know that his "self" is neither his emotion nor his mind, but rather that the center of his consciousness judges *both*. Pastoral healing leads others not to work *from* their emotions and mind, but to work *on* them *to begin with*.

Regarding the *atmosphere* in which this can happen, however, it is St. Paul who best speaks: "to the weak I became weak, that I may win the weak" (1 Cor. 9:22). About the image in which the pastor does this: "For we have not a high priest who is unable to sympathize [συμπαθέω] with our weakness" (Heb. 4:15).

Therefore, the pastor, in his very person, must create this atmosphere of acceptance in which the "sin is hated but not the sinner," in which, although "we have done no good deed upon the earth" and are "sinful and unworthy servants," we can still have the "boldness to draw near" (Anaphora of St. Basil's Liturgy).

It is in this atmosphere of acceptance, then, that we lead people to true liberation from their selves. Thus Isaiah speaks to the pastoral task: "The Lord has anointed me to bring good tidings to the afflicted; he has sent me to bind up the brokenhearted, to proclaim liberty to the captives" (61:1).

[10]Sidney Jourard, *The Transparent Self: Self-Disclosure and Well Being* (Princeton, N. J.: Van Nostrand, 1964) 5.
[11]Ibid., p. 9.

Healing and Guilt. Having established the need for an atmosphere of acceptance, we must specifically deal with the problem of *guilt*. We have already said much regarding this, and it shows that the healing of guilt is deeply connected with all the foregoing points.

There are two major points, however, which must be clarified regarding how the pastor must see the problem of guilt and healing as distinct from a more secular view. First, the transaction between the person and God (as mediated by the priest) asks the question of guilt and responsibility *before his Creator*. There is here a meaning beyond the moment, beyond adjustment, and into the ultimate range of hope and salvation. And second, the healing comes from beyond the person of the pastor, i.e., it is not limited to his helpful word.

This being true, every pastor must know that there is, first, *real* guilt, which is a consequence of a *misused freedom*; secondly, a *wrong* guilt, in which one feels guilty out of proportion to reality; and thirdly, the *consequences of guilt*, which sometimes even have a strong effect on our *physical* being (which demonstrates the *holistic* need for repentance and absolution).

The naive picture of "love alone" does not work. The paranoid person, for example, cannot be helped by offering only sympathy and a kind word. We are not, in this case, really "feeding the hungry person," but feeding his disease. In a like manner, the healing of guilt will not be effected until one comes to terms with that which is causing the guilt; accountability is an obvious pastoral inclusion. Love in pastoral healing obviously needs some balance of understanding exactly what is at hand.

This "understanding of what is at hand," however, does not change the purpose of the pastoral concern, since it is still an "agapic" model. But this love is the affirmation of the existence of the other, i.e., that he *be* rather than *not* be (which can only begin what he *can* be). Such an "agapic" model cannot be reached in the atmosphere of the "intellectualizers" of the Enlightenment, who were "detached" (e.g., Voltaire) and more above the battle than in it, who possessed more a love of the *idea about* humanity rather than a love of persons as persons. It can only be realized in the love of Jesus Christ, who responds to the hands that reach out for the hem of His garment.

This question of healing and guilt brings into focus the need for another clarification. The Christian ideal of life envisions something higher than freedom from anguish. This goal cannot be merely a perfectly adjusted self; in fact, to live in the love of God means precisely to accept the risk of life and the threats to "peace of mind." We are healed, or in other words, set free of our burdens, simply to assume more important and new burdens. We are healed *for others* (a radical distinction from the secular image of healing).

The story of sin, which our self knows and feels, is the very story of *real* guilt. To be healed of guilt in a pastoral perspective is to know the story of sin in its existential meaning. This story, for the pastor, can include (1) *unbelief* and the lack of trust in God; (2) ὕβρις, or the self-elevation (pride) of man as usurper of God's place; and (3) *lust*, the feeding of our own gratifications. Not wishing here to do the work of the systematic theologian, I merely mention them as those pastoral dimensions in which *real* guilt must be seen. Sin, in this perspective, is a violation of our essential nature—a state of inner dividedness—a "war" with self and God. It is a veritable definition of the genesis of guilt, and for healing, it needs those elements we have mentioned in the previous points (and will not repeat here), i.e., in our inner resources, in the atmosphere of acceptance.

The Pastor Himself as a Source of Healing

I am not foolish enough to believe or pretend that this is where in all cases (or even in many cases!) the Orthodox pastor is. One could be cynical and say, "this is not the way things are." However, great fires begin with small flames, and if the process cannot begin in the training of pastors, i.e., in Orthodox seminary training, then where can it begin? Will we always be satisfied with what is, neglecting the straining toward the ought? "Healers" are what we must be!

This is so because of those crises with which we come into contact. We have barely touched the surface in the points hitherto developed—which predominantly dealt only with the individual dimensions. I am convinced, however, that the meaning of each point easily attaches itself to other dimensions—e.g., marital problems, community problems, etc. What pastor does not know these crises? Here a couple is eager for an approaching wedding, there a couple lives in the nightmare of marital brokenness and bitterness. Here parents rejoice at the birth of a new baby, there they weep over a dying child. Here a young woman receives a scholarship to study, there one fails entrance. Here a young child awaits a summer vacation, there an old person awaits nothing but a lonely life, asking why death does not come as a deliverance. Joy and sorrow, sickness and health, plenty and want—this kaleidoscopic montage of experience is the area in which the pastor does his shepherding.

In any one of these many possibilities, the pastor must be aware of many traps and pitfalls. This he must do if he will be himself a source of healing. This is our third and last major concern.

Congruence of the Pastor. We have said that the pastor, in terms of healing, must reflect what God Himself has done for us, that He has accepted us while not approving of all we have done, that He came to us in all our sin because human nature is "very good." We must project what the kerygma proclaims: *Deus pro nobis*, God for us! Each act of the pastor-in-relationship *implicitly* bears what the kerygma *explicitly* declares!

An important aspect of our reflecting God's concern and healing is that of *congruence*. We have learned that God does not cease to be Himself in the midst of His sharing in the human existence. God continues to be at one with Himself, being "He who is"; He never loses His inner *unity* and *integrity*. This is the divine congruence. The pastor reflects this truth in his own dealing as he relates to the suffering and sin of another, yet *remains who he is*. The parishioner must sense the inner congruence of the pastor. He must know that he is in the presence of one who is in touch with himself and his own life, even as he encounters the other's enstrangement.

I pointed earlier to presence and person of the pastor, and I must again. This is because being in the very presence of a congruent person, one who *is* who he is and *knows* who he is, undoubtedly has a healing possibility: he can be a handle onto which I can hold; he can be the otherness that I need; he can remain separate and not so identified with me as to lose that self-congruence. (One does not and *should* not embody fear to share another's fear!) Here Robert Katz speaks the truth as he refers to "empathy" as a "dialectic between the actual me and the me which is identified with the other person ... a paradoxical process in which we are at the same time fully absorbed in the identity of the other and yet capable of an experience of ourselves as separate personalities."[12] The pastor learns to share the experience, i.e., "co-suffers," yet remains distinctively himself as "other." Thus, although participating, he never negates his own identity. This paradigm is learned in the meaning of God's incarnation in Christ; God "healed" us by becoming man (*vere homo*), but because He also remained God (*vere Deus*).

Covenant Ontology. Any Orthodox priest should identify with Thomas Oden's use of the term "covenant ontology." This term, with which he describes certain pastoral assumptions of healing, I would like to use in an Orthodox perspective. What Oden means by these two words is "a study of being which sees being as existing in covenant, and the covenant of God as the center and circumference of being."[13] If "ontology" means the study of human existence, i.e., man's knowing, being, feeling, deciding and doing, and "covenant" means the relationship that God has chosen for us (and not that we have chosen for Him!), then the pastor has to see "healing" precisely in this context. "They shall be my people, and I will be their God" (Jer. 32:28).

[12]Robert Katz, *Empathy: Its Nature and Uses* (Toronto: Collier-Macmillan, 1963) 157.
[13]Oden, p. 78.

Without this "covenant ontology," what kind of healing will we do? To what end? With what *meaning*? Here we see the "analogy of faith" (*analogia fidei*) as radically different from the secular model. Healing is set in what we see God doing, i.e., the pastor is to do what God has done in His covenant with the world. Oden, in his "covenant ontology," speaks of a fivefold healing process which rests in such a covenant: "The healing process involves a fivefold development which may be seen as analogous to five aspects of the activity of God ... corresponding also to five basic dimensions of a phenomenology of human existence: knowing, being, feeling, deciding and doing."[14]

In his human and limited capacity, if the pastor will "heal," it will be within his alignment with God's "knowing, being, feeling, deciding and doing." Of course, as Orthodox we know that we can never completely do this because of our very humanity and God's incomprehensibility. But we can do this as far as we *can*, and of course, that is where the Church as God's body in the world enters; we can heal within these five dimensions according to the "mind of the Church." Thus, our healing in the covenant with God is precisely in our covenant with the Church.

If I could chart this healing process in covenant ontology, again from an Orthodox perspective, it would look like the table on the following page. At each dimension, it is a case of we pastors being who we are because God is who He is; our helping reflects His helping. Any healing that we mediate is His very own.

Conclusion: When We Fail

In attempting to explore the synthesis of personal wholeness through the pastoral dimensions of healing, we have been discovering first scriptural and contemporary "linkage"; secondly, the *praxis* of healing (in terms of healing and human experience, healing and other selves, healing through inner resources and acceptance, healing and guilt); and finally, the

[14]Ibid., p. 80.

PASTORAL HEALING IN COVENANT ONTOLOGY

Dimensions of Human Existence	Healing Process Of Pastor	In Relation To God
Undertanding (Cognitive)	Empathetic Understanding	In Covenant
Being (Ontic)	Congruence	In Covenant
Feeling (Emotive)	Acceptance	In Covenant
Willing (Volitional)	Guidance	In Covenant
Acting (Relational)	Respect For Other	In Covenant

pastor himself as a source of healing (in terms of the congruence of the pastor and covenant ontology). There are, as mentioned at the outset, other subjects, e.g., in marriage, geriatrics, etc., which could be studied with probably a more scientific approach. Hopefully, we have opened some doors in understanding these other areas also.

The only problem left is that we may—and often *will*—fail to heal. But I will insist that in our all-too-human failings, God may still heal. When we *fail*, then we turn for hope to the example of Job. Job's pleadings are like a theorem: he is innocent and struck down with misfortune and illness. The Almighty God does not answer his plea for healing. Is God unjust?

An upright and God-fearing man, Job has lost everything: his cattle and asses, his servants and camels, and then his sons and daughters. As if that is not enough, he falls sick with "sore boils from the sole of his foot to the crown" (2:7). And then comes the sarcasm of his wife and "curious" friends.

But as we hear God's voice, another deeper *meaning*

comes: "Where were you when I laid the foundation of the earth?" (Job 38:41) Besides the mystery of God's creative work, Job discovers his humanity and remembers that "man is born into trouble" (5:7)—neither taken out of the world nor removed from contact with disease and evil, but *greeted at that very point* with God's care. For the Christian, God's care is demonstrated in the incarnation. Could not our response to the human failure to heal then be: "Behold, I am of small account; what shall I answer thee? I lay my hand upon my mouth!" (Job 40:4)

Date